THE SECRET
OF MARY

WITH PREPARATION FOR
TOTAL CONSECRATION

SAINT LOUIS DE MONTFORT

CATHOLIC WAY
PUBLISHING

CONTENTS

PRAYERS

ABOUT SAINT LOUIS DE MONTFORT

St. Louis Marie Grignion de la Bacheleraie, who abandoned his family name for that of his birthplace, was born on January 31, 1673 in the little town of Montfort-la-Canne, which is located in Brittany, France. He studied for the priesthood at St. Sulpice in Paris, having made the 200-mile journey there on foot. He was ordained a priest in 1700, at the age of 27.

St. Louis De Montfort had wanted to become a missionary in Canada, but he was advised to remain in France. . There he traveled around the western part of the country, from diocese to diocese and from parish to parish, instructing the people, preaching, helping the poor, hearing confessions, giving retreats, opening schools and rebuilding church buildings. His labors were almost miraculously fruitful. He stated that never did a sinner resist after being touched by him with a Rosary.

But because he encountered great opposition from religious authorities—in particular, being forbidden by the Bishop of Poitiers to preach in his diocese—he decided to travel to Rome to ask the Holy Father if he was doing God's Will and whether he should continue as before. St. Louis De Montfort walked to Rome—a thousand miles—and put his case to

Pope Clement XI. The Pope told him to continue his traveling missionary work and named him Missionary Apostolic, but told him always to be sure to work under obedience to the diocesan authorities.

One of St. Louis De Montfort's greatest problems was the opposition he encountered from propagators of the Jansenist .heresy, which was then very active in France. The Jansenists spread an atmosphere of harshness and moral rigorism, claiming that human nature was radically corrupted by Original Sin . The Jansenists denied that God's mercy is available to all, and they allowed only infrequent reception of the Sacraments of Penance and the Holy Eucharist, and only after long and severe preparation—with Holy Communion being looked upon as a reward rather than a remedy. Also, they taught that God should always be addressed with fear and trembling. These tenets resembled those of Calvinism.

Although Jansenism had been condemned by the Church twice even before St. Louis De Montfort's birth, its teachings continued to spread and to influence people for a century. In contrast, St. Louis De Montfort preached confidence in Mary and union with her Divine Son.

St. Louis De Montfort founded two religious orders: the Daughters of Wisdom, begun in 1703 from a number of poor and afflicted girls at the Hospital of Poitiers, where he was temporary chaplain, and the Missionaries of the Company of Mary , founded in 1715. The Brothers of St. Gabriel, a teaching order, also claim St. Louis De Montfort as their spiritual father.

St. Louis De Montfort left several writings, the most famous being *The Secret of the Rosary, True Devotion to Mary,* and *The Secret of Mary.* These books were based on sermons he had given when traveling around France. By spreading devotion to the Blessed Virgin Mary, St. Louis De Montfort was teaching souls to love the devil's great enemy. At the Saint's beatification investigation, many witnesses testified that during his life they had heard struggles between him and the devil, including the sound of fist blows and the swish of whips.

St. Louis De Montfort exhausted his great physical strength by his apostolic labors. On his death-bed in Saint-Laurent-sur-Sevre, at age 43, he kissed the Crucifix and a statue of the Blessed Mother. Apparently speaking to the devil, he exclaimed: "In vain do you attack me; I am between Jesus and Mary! I have finished my course: All is over. I shall sin no more!" Then he died peacefully on April 28, 1716. His feast day is April 28, the day of his birth in Heaven. St. Louis De Montfort's writings were examined by the Holy See, which pronounced that there was nothing in them to hinder his beatification and canonization. He was canonized in 1947.

Part I

DOCTRINE OF THE HOLY SLAVERY

"Mary is the admirable echo of God. When we say, 'Mary,' she answers, 'God.' When, with St. Elizabeth, we call her 'Blessed, ' she glorifies God."—St. Louis De Montfort

INTRODUCTION

A SECRET OF SANCTITY

CONDITIONS

1. Predestinate soul, here is a secret the Most High has taught me, which I have not been able to find in any book, old or new.[1] I confide it to you, by the inspiration of the Holy Ghost, on condition:

That you communicate it only to those who deserve it by their prayers, their alms-deeds and mortifications, by the

---

[1] The holy slavery of Jesus in Mary was known, no doubt, before St. Louis De Montfort's time; yet he rightly calls this devotion *a secret:* first, because there lies in it, as in all things supernatural, a hidden treasure which grace alone can help us to find and utilize; secondly, because there are but few souls that enter into the spirit of this devotion and go beyond its exterior practices. Again, as no one had as yet thoroughly explained this devotion nor shaped it into a definite method of spiritual life, St. Louis De Montfort could say of a truth, "I have not been able to find this secret in any book, old or new."

persecutions they suffer, by their detachment from the world and their zeal for the salvation of souls.[2]

That you make use of it for your personal sanctification and salvation, for this secret works its effect in a soul only in proportion to the use made of it. beware, then, of remaining inactive while possessing my secret; it would turn into a poison and be your condemnation.[3]

That you thank God all the days of your life for the grace He has given you to know a secret you do not deserve to know. As you go on making use of this secret in the ordinary actions of your life, you will comprehend its value and its excellence, which at first you will not fully understand because of your

---

[2] These words show how highly St. Louis De Montfort esteemed this devotion. As there are professional secrets committed only to men who know how to appreciate and exploit them, so this secret of sanctity must be entrusted only to such souls as truly concern themselves with their perfection; and following the recommendation of Our Lord not to profane holy things , De Montfort preserves this secret with a holy jealousy that denotes respect for Divine things.

[3] "This solemn warning of the Saint is an application of the Parable of the Talents reported in Matthew 25. The unfaithful servant buried the talent he received and was condemned by the Master for his culpable negligence and for his disdain for the gifts of God. It is also a condemnation of the passivity or inertia taught by the false spirituality of Quietism or semi-Quietism that existed in St. De Montfort's time and that was condemned by Rome. The Saint does not mean that one is obliged to follow his plan of spiritual life in order to be saved, for in his *Treatise on the True Devotion to Mary,* which is a development of the *Secret of Mary,* he explicitly says that we can attain Divine union by other roads, but that his method is an EASY, SHORT, PERFECT and SECURE WAY that leads us to union with Our Lord."

many and grievous sins and because of your secret attachment to self.[4]

2. Before you read any further, lest you should be carried away by a too eager and natural desire to know this truth, kneel down and say devoutly the Ave Maris Stella[5] and the Veni Creator,[6] in order to understand and appreciate this Divine mystery.[7]

As I have not much time for writing, nor you for reading, I shall say everything as briefly as possible.

---

[4] These words contain three important counsels: 1) This devotion must be practiced in the ordinary course of life as well as in the most important actions. 2) Only when we steadily persevere in it, and not merely try it for a few weeks, shall we be able to judge of its excellence and know its fruit. 3) It is necessary to remove all hindrances to this devotion, namely, sin and secret affection for that which is sinful.

[5] Ave Maris Stella

[6] Veni Creator.

[7] Let us not make light of this recommendation. It is an important one. If many persons do not become acquainted with the secret of this devotion, it is because they forget that in order to be allowed to enter this "Garden Enclosed," as Mary is called, they must entreat the Holy Ghost, "Who searcheth all things, yea, the deep things of God" , to grant them that favor.

THE NECESSITY OF SANCTIFYING OURSELVES

THE WILL OF GOD

3. Faithful soul, living image of God, redeemed by the Precious Blood of Jesus Christ, it is the will of God that you be holy like Him in this life and glorious like Him in the next. Your sure vocation is the acquisition of the holiness of God, and unless all your thoughts and words and actions, all the sufferings and events of your life tend to that end, you are resisting God by not doing that for which He has created you and is now preserving you.[8] Oh, what an admirable work! To change that which is dust into light, to make pure that which is unclean, holy that which is sinful, to make the creature like its Creator, man like God! Admirable work, I repeat, but difficult in itself, and impossible to mere nature; only God by His grace, by His abundant and extraordinary grace, can accomplish it. Even the creation of the whole world is not so great a masterpiece as this.

---

[8] Those who begin this devotion are here reminded of the recommendation of the masters of the spiritual life, namely, that the interior life must be their chief concern. They must be determined to obtain good results bought with the price of sacrifice. Compare these words with St. Louis De Montfort's advice on cultivating.

MEANS OF SANCTIFICATION

4. Predestinate soul, how are you to do it? What means will you choose to reach the height to which God calls you? The means of salvation and sanctification are known to all; they are laid down in the Gospel, explained by the masters of the spiritual life, practiced by the Saints, and necessary to all who wish to be saved and to attain perfection. They are humility of heart, continual prayer, mortification in all things, abandonment to Divine Providence and conformity to the will of God.

5. To practice all these means of salvation and sanctification, the grace of God is absolutely necessary. No one can doubt that God gives His grace to all, in a more or less abundant measure. I say in a more or less abundant measure, for God, although infinitely good, does not give equal grace to all, yet to each soul He gives sufficient grace.

The faithful soul will, with great grace, perform a great action, and with less grace a lesser action. It is the value and the excellence of the grace bestowed by God and corresponded to by the soul that gives to our actions their value and their excellence. These principles are certain.

AN EASY MEANS

6. It all comes to this, then: that you should find an easy means for obtaining from God the grace necessary to make you holy; and this means I wish to make known to you. Now, I say that to find this grace of God, *we must find Mary.*[9]

---

[9] This is characteristic of St. Louis De Montfort's devotion and makes it a special method of spiritual life.

OUR SANCTIFICATION THROUGH
MARY, A NECESSARY MEANS[10]

MARY ALONE HAS FOUND GRACE WITH GOD

7. Mary alone has found grace with God, both for herself and for every man in particular. The patriarchs and prophets and all the Saints of the Old Law were not able to find that grace.

MOTHER OF GRACE

8. Mary gave being and life to the Author of all grace, and that is why she is called the Mother of Grace.

MARY HAS RECEIVED THE PLENITUDE OF GRACE

9. God the Father, from Whom every perfect gift and all grace come, as from its essential source, has given all graces to Mary by giving her His Son, so that, as St. Bernard says,

---

[10] The reasons given here to prove that Mary is the most perfect means for finding Jesus are a condensed treatise on Mariology. If the faithful meditate on these points, they will come to understand the function assigned to Our Lady, by virtue of her Divine maternity, in the mystery of the Incarnation and now in the whole Church.

"With His Son and in Him, God has given His Will to Mary."

UNIVERSAL TREASURER OF GOD'S GRACES

10. God has entrusted Mary with the keeping, the administration and distribution of all His graces, so that all His graces and gifts pass through her hands; and , as St. Bernardine teaches, Mary gives to whom she wills, the way she wills, when she wills and as much as she wills, the graces of the Eternal Father, the virtues of Jesus Christ and the gifts of the Holy Ghost.

MOTHER OF GOD'S CHILDREN

11. As in the order of nature a child must have a father and a mother, so likewise in the order of grace, a true child of the Church must have God for his Father and Mary for his Mother; and if anyone should glory in having God for his Father and yet has not the love of a true child for Mary, he is a deceiver, and the only father he has is the devil.

MARY FORMS THE MEMBERS OF JESUS

12. Since Mary has formed Jesus Christ, the Head of the elect, it is also her office to form the members of that Head, that is to say, all true Christians; for a mother does not form the head without the members, nor the members without the head. Whoever, therefore, wishes to be a member of Jesus Christ, full of grace and truth, must be formed in Mary by means of the grace of Jesus Christ, which she possesses in its

fullness, in order to communicate it fully to her children, the true members of Jesus Christ.[11]

THROUGH HER THE HOLY GHOST PRODUCES THE ELECT

13. As the Holy Ghost has espoused Mary and has produced in her, by her and from her, His masterpiece, Jesus Christ, the Word Incarnate, and has never repudiated His spouse, so He now continues to produce the elect, in her and by her, in a mysterious but real manner.

MARY NOURISHES SOULS AND GIVES THEM GROWTH IN GOD

14. Mary has received a special office and power over our souls in order to nourish them and give them growth in God. St. Augustine even says that, during their present life, all the elect are hidden in Mary's womb and that they are not truly born until the Blessed Mother brings them forth to life eternal. Consequently, just as the child draws all its nourishment from the mother, who gives it in proportion to the child's weakness, in like manner do the elect draw all their spiritual nourishment and strength from Mary.

---

[11] Conclude from this that we call Mary our Mother not because of mere feelings of piety and gratitude awakened in us by the conviction that she loves and protects us, but because she is our Mother in the spiritual order as truly as she is the Mother of Christ in the natural order. The spiritual motherhood of Mary, a consequence of her Divine motherhood, is one of the truths on which the True Devotion of St. Louis De Montfort is founded.

MARY DWELLS IN THE ELECT

15. It is to Mary that God the Father said: "My daughter, let thy dwelling be in Jacob," that is, in My elect, prefigured by Jacob. It is to Mary that God the Son said: "My dear Mother, in Israel is thine inheritance," that is, in the elect. And it is to Mary that the Holy Ghost said: "Take root, My faithful spouse, in My elect." Whoever, then, is elect and predestinate has the Blessed Virgin with him, dwelling in his soul,[12] and he will allow her to plant there the roots of profound humility, of ardent charity and of every virtue.

MARY FORMS JESUS IN US A LIVING MOLD OF GOD

16. St. Augustine calls Mary the living "mold of God," and that indeed she is; for it was in her alone that God was made a true man without losing any feature of the Godhead, and it is also in her alone that man can be truly formed Into God,

---

[12] This abode of Mary in our soul may be explained in the following manner: Her presence in us cannot be compared to that of God living in our soul by Sanctifying Grace and thus making us partakers of His Divine life. Neither must we believe that Mary is bodily present in our soul. Some have wrongfully charged St. Louis De Montfort with inferring the omnipresence of Mary. But let us bear in mind Mary's privilege of being truly the Mother of God . As a consequence of that privilege, Mary beholds our souls in a universal manner and more excellently than the Saints and Angels do in their Heavenly glory, and she is with us really, individually, intimately. Thus, we are morally present to her, and she is morally present to us, because by her prayers, her attention and her influence she cooperates with the Holy Ghost in forming Jesus in our souls. By way of comparison, we might say that Mary is present in our souls as the sun is present in a room by its light and warmth, even though it is not there itself.

in so far as that is possible for human nature, by the grace of Jesus Christ.

A sculptor has two ways of making a lifelike statue or figure: He may carve the figure out of some hard, shapeless material, using for this purpose his professional skill and knowledge, his strength and the necessary instruments, or he may cast it in a mold. The first manner is long and difficult and subject to many mishaps; a single blow of the hammer or the chisel, awkwardly given, may spoil the whole work. The second is short, easy and smooth; it requires but little work and slight expense, provided the mold be perfect and made to reproduce the figure exactly; provided, moreover, the material used offer no resistance to the hand of the artist.[13]

A PERFECT MOLD

17. Mary is the great mold of God, made by the Holy Ghost to form a true God-Man by the Hypostatic Union and to form also a man-God by grace. In that mold none of the features of the Godhead is wanting. Whoever is cast in it, and allows himself to be molded, receives all the features of Jesus Christ, true God. The work is done gently, in a manner proportioned to human weakness, without much pain or labor, in a sure manner, free from all illusion, for where Mary is the devil has never had and never will have access; finally, it is done in a holy and spotless manner, without a shadow of the least stain of sin.

---

[13] Therefore great docility is required on our part if we would be "formed quickly, easily and gently." This comparison of the mold explains very well the interior practice of this devotion. The devotion consists essentially in one single act which, under various forms and conditions, we apply to our whole life, both interior and exterior. Such is the simplicity of St. Louis De Montfort's method.

WELL-MOLTEN SOULS

18. Oh what a difference between a soul which has been formed in Christ by the ordinary ways of those who, like the sculptor, trust in their own skill 'and ingenuity, and a soul thoroughly tractable, entirely detached and well-molten, which, without trusting to its own skill, casts itself into Mary, there to be molded by the Holy Ghost. How many stains and defects and illusions, how much darkness and how much human nature is there in the former; and oh how pure, how Heavenly and how Christlike is the latter!

PARADISE AND WORLD OF GOD

19. There does not exist and never will exist a creature in whom God, either within or without Himself, is so highly exalted as He is in the most Blessed Virgin Mary, not excepting the Saints or the Cherubim or the highest Seraphim in Paradise. Mary is the paradise of God and His unspeakable world, into which the Son of God has come to work His wonders, to watch over it and to take His delight in it. God has made a world for wayfaring man, which is that world in which we dwell; He has made one for man in his glorified state, which is Heaven; and He has made one for Himself, which He has called Mary. It is a world unknown to most mortals here below and incomprehensible even to the Angels and Blessed in Heaven above, who, seeing God so highly exalted above them all and so deeply hidden in Mary, His world, are filled with admiration and unceasingly exclaim: "Holy, Holy, Holy."

GOD ALONE IN HER

20. Happy, a thousand times happy, is the soul here below to which the Holy Ghost reveals the Secret of Mary in order

that it may come to know her; to which He opens the "Garden Enclosed" , that it may enter into it; to which He gives access to that "Fountain Sealed," that it may draw from it and drink deep draughts of the living waters of grace! That soul will find God alone in His most amiable creature. It will find God infinitely holy and exalted, yet at the same time adapting Himself to its own weakness. Since God is present everywhere, He may be found everywhere, even in Hell, but nowhere do we creatures find Him nearer to us and more adapted to our weakness than in Mary, since it was for that end that He came and dwelt in her. Everywhere else He is the Bread of the strong, the Bread of the Angels, but in Mary He is the Bread of children.[14]

NO HINDRANCE TO OUR UNION WITH GOD

21. Let us not imagine, then, as some do who are misled by erroneous teachings, that Mary, being a creature, is a hindrance to our union with the Creator. It is no longer Mary who lives, it is Jesus Christ, it is God alone who lives in her. Her transformation into God surpasses that of St. Paul and of the other Saints more than the heavens surpass the earth by their height. Mary is made for God alone, and far from ever detaining a soul in herself, she casts the soul upon God

---

[14] This beautiful expression interprets the invitation of Divine Wisdom: "Come, eat the bread and drink the wine which I have mingled for you." . It also accounts for the unexpected graces which this devotion draws upon those who persevere in its practice. Note that this method of spiritual formation is practically the same as the education given by a mother to her child. In ourselves we experience the infirmities and the wants of infancy, in Mary we find the strong and never wearied love of a mother. All that we have to do is to abandon ourselves to Mary and to remain dependent on her in all things, just like children.

and unites it with Him so much the more perfectly as the soul is more perfectly united to her. Mary is the admirable echo of God. When we say, "Mary," she answers, "God." When, with St. Elizabeth, we call her "Blessed," she glorifies God. If the falsely enlightened, whom the devil has so miserably disillusioned, even in prayer, had known how to find Mary, and through her to find Jesus, and through Jesus, God the Father, they would not have had such terrible falls. The Saints tell us that when we have once found Mary, and through Mary, Jesus, and through Jesus, God the Father, we have found all good. He who says all excepts nothing: all grace and all friendship with God, all safety from God's enemies, all truth to crush falsehoods, all facility to overcome difficulties in the way of salvation, all comfort and all joy amidst the bitterness of life.

SHE IMPARTS THE GRACE TO CARRY CROSSES

22. This does not mean that he who has found Mary by a true devotion will be exempt from crosses and sufferings.[15] Far from it; he is more besieged by them than others are, because Mary, the Mother of the living, gives to all her children portions of the Tree of Life, which is the Cross of Jesus. But along with their crosses she also imparts the grace to carry them patiently and even cheerfully; and thus it is that the crosses which she lays upon those who belong to her are rather steeped in sweetness than filled with bitterness. If

---

[15] St. Louis De Montfort has explained that his true devotion is an easy means of sanctification, yet he wishes to guard us against the common illusion that his method exempts us from spiritual labor and sufferings. He is himself a striking example of the manly education which Mary, the valiant woman, gives to her children, as well as of the love of Jesus crucified which she enkindles in their hearts.

for a while her children feel the bitterness of the cup which one must needs drink in order to be the friend of God, the consolation and joy which this good Mother sends after the trial encourage them exceedingly to carry still heavier and more painful crosses.

CONCLUSION

23. The difficulty, then, is to find really and truly the most Blessed Virgin Mary in order to find all abundant grace. God, being the absolute Master, can confer directly by Himself that which He usually grants only through Mary. It would even be rash to deny that sometimes He does so.

Nevertheless, St. Thomas teaches that in the order of grace, established by Divine Wisdom, God ordinarily communicates Himself to men only through Mary. Therefore, if we would go up to Him and be united with Him, we must use the same means He used to come down to us, to be made man and to impart His graces to us. That means is a true devotion to our Blessed Lady.

OUR SANCTIFICATION BY THE PERFECT
DEVOTION TO THE BLESSED SLAVERY OF LOVE

24. There are several true devotions to Our Lady: here I do not speak of those that are false.

1. DEVOTION WITHOUT SPECIAL PRACTICES

25. The first consists in fulfilling our Christian duties, avoiding mortal sin, acting more out of love than fear, praying to Our Lady now and then, honoring her as the Mother of God, yet without having any special devotion to her.

2. DEVOTION WITH SPECIAL PRACTICES

26. The second consists in entertaining for Our Lady more perfect feelings of esteem and love, of confidence and veneration. It leads us to join the Confraternities of the Holy Rosary and of the Scapular, to recite the five decades or the fifteen decades of the Rosary, to honor Mary's images and altars, to publish her praises and to enroll ourselves in her

sodalities.[16] This devotion is good, holy and praiseworthy, if we keep ourselves free from sin; but it is not so perfect as the next, nor so efficient in severing our soul from creatures or in detaching us from ourselves, in order to be united with Jesus Christ.

3. THE PERFECT DEVOTION: THE HOLY SLAVERY OF LOVE

27. The third devotion to Our Lady, known and practiced by very few persons, is the one I am now about to disclose to you, predestinate soul.

---

[16] All such devotions, remarks St. Louis De Montfort elsewhere, include but a limited number of devout practices and take up but a part of our daily life, while the one he proposes embraces our whole life and divests us of all things.

THE NATURE AND SCOPE OF THIS DEVOTION

NATURE

28. It consists in giving oneself entirely and as a slave to Mary, and to Jesus through Mary; and after that to do all that we do, with Mary, in Mary, through Mary and for Mary.[17] I shall now explain these words.

SCOPE: TOTAL SURRENDER

29. We should choose a special feast-day on which to give, consecrate and sacrifice to Mary voluntarily, lovingly and without constraint, entirely and without reserve: our body and soul, our exterior property, such as house, family and

---

[17] We must, therefore, note two things in this devotion: first, an *act* of total consecration to Jesus through Mary; and secondly, a *state* of being consecrated. That state consists in the permanent disposition of living and acting habitually in dependence on Mary; and that is called the spirit or the interior part of this consecration. This practice, although it embraces our entire life, appears so small and trifling at first glance, that St. Louis De Montfort has justly compared it to the mustard seed. But one comes to realize its vital energy and its wonderful effects when it has grown strong by persistent exercise.

income; and also our interior and spiritual possessions; namely, our merits, graces, virtues and satisfactions.[18]

It should be observed here that by this devotion the soul sacrifices to Jesus, through Mary, all that it holds most dear, things of which even no religious order would require the sacrifice; namely, the right to dispose of ourselves, of the value of our prayers and alms, of our mortifications and satisfactions. The soul leaves everything to be freely disposed of by Our Lady so that she may apply it all according to her own will for the greater glory of God, which she alone knows perfectly.

SURRENDER OF THE VALUE OF OUR GOOD WORKS

30. We leave to her disposal all the satisfactory and impetratory value of our good works, so that after we have made the sacrifice of them—although not by vow—we are no longer the masters of any good works we may do; but Our Lady may apply them, sometimes for the relief or the deliverance of a soul in Purgatory, sometimes for the conversion of a poor sinner, etc.[19]

---

[18] These words show us the far-reaching effect of this consecration, which St. Louis De Montfort calls a perfect renewal of the Baptismal vows; and, indeed, in making it we give ourselves anew to Jesus Christ, Our Lord, through the hands of Mary.

[19] It may not be amiss to give here a short explanation of the Heroic Act of Charity, and to point out in what it differs from this act of consecration.

According to a definition of the Sacred Congregation of Indulgences , the Heroic Act of Charily consists in this: that a member of the Church Militant offers to God, for the souls in Purgatory, all the satisfactory works which he will perform during his lifetime and also all the suffrages which may accrue to him after his death.

31. By this devotion we also place our merits in the hands of
Our Lady, but only that she may preserve, augment and
embellish them, because we cannot communicate to one
another either the merits of sanctifying grace or those of
glory. However, we give her all our prayers and good works,
inasmuch as they have an impetratory and satisfactory value,
that she may distribute and apply them to whom she pleases.
If, after having thus consecrated ourselves to Our Lady, we
desire to relieve a Soul in Purgatory, to save a sinner, or to
assist a friend by our prayers, our alms-deeds, our mortifications and sacrifices, we must humbly ask it of Our Lady,
abiding, however, by her decision, which remains unknown
to us; and we must be fully persuaded that the value of our
actions, being dispensed by the same hand which God Himself makes use of to distribute to us His graces and gifts,
cannot fail to be applied for His greater glory.

By the Act of Consecration to Jesus through Mary as taught by St.
Louis De Montfort, we give to Our Lady not only the satisfactory
works of our life, but all else, nothing excepted. The use to be made
of our good works and satisfactions is not determined by us, as it is
in the Heroic Act, but it is left to Mary's intention and will. In his
Act of Consecration, St. Louis De Montfort does not seem to
comprise directly the suffrages which may accrue to us in Purgatory, but indirectly they are implied: "I leave to thee . . . all that
belongs to me . . . in time and in eternity."
Neither the Heroic Act nor our Act of Consecration implies a vow,
yet both may be made with a vow, if discretion and sound judgment are not lacking in making such a solemn promise to God.

THREE KINDS OF SLAVERY

32. I have said that this devotion consists in giving ourselves to Mary as slaves.[20] But notice that there are three kinds of slavery. The first is the slavery of nature; in this sense all men, good and bad alike, are slaves of God. The second is the slavery of constraint; the devils and the damned are slaves of God in this second sense. The third is the slavery of love and of free will; and this is the one by which we must consecrate ourselves to God through Mary. It is the most perfect way for us human creatures to give ourselves to God our Creator.

SERVANT AND SLAVE

33. Notice again, that there is a great difference between a servant and a slave. A servant claims wages for his services; a slave has a right to none. A servant is free to leave his master when he likes—he serves him only for a time; a slave belongs to his master for life and has no right to leave him. A servant does not give to his master the right of life and death over him; a slave gives himself up entirely, so that his master can

---

[20] These words show us the true nature of this consecration. By making it we place ourselves in a state in which we are owned by Jesus and Mary and are totally dependent on Their will. Now that is the nature and the condition of a slave. But to remove the idea of there being any degradation or tyrannical violence in this noble servitude, St. Louis De Montfort explains that it is a voluntary slavery, full of honor and of love, giving us the liberty of the true children of God.

There is then no reason for being scared or repelled by the words "slave" and "slavery." Consider the *state,* not the *word* which expresses the state of total, of lasting and disinterested subjection and dependence on the Master through the Mother. One may ask why not use other words? It is because there are none to express adequately this special state of consecration.

put him to death without being molested by the law. It is easily seen, then, that he who is a slave by constraint is rigorously dependent on his master. Strictly speaking, a man must be dependent in that sense only on his Creator. Hence, we do not find that kind of slavery among Christians, but only among pagans.

HAPPINESS OF THE SLAVE OF LOVE

34. But happy and a thousand times happy is the generous soul that consecrates itself entirely to Jesus through Mary as a slave of love after it has shaken off by Baptism the tyrannical slavery of the devil!

EXCELLENCE OF THE HOLY SLAVERY OF LOVE

I should require much supernatural light to describe perfectly the excellence of this practice.

I shall content myself with these few remarks.

IMITATION OF THE TRINITY

35. To give ourselves to Jesus through Mary is to imitate God the Father, Who has given us His Son only through Mary, and Who communicates to us His grace only through Mary. It is to imitate God the Son, Who has come to us only through Mary, and Who, "by giving us an example, that as He has done, so we do also" , has urged us to go to Him by the same means by which He has come to us—that is, through Mary. It is to imitate the Holy Ghost, Who bestows His graces and gifts upon us only through Mary. "Is it not fitting," asks St. Bernard, "that grace should return to its Author by the same channel which conveyed it to us?"

IT HONORS JESUS

36. To go to Jesus through Mary is truly to honor Jesus Christ, for it denotes that we do not esteem ourselves worthy of approaching His infinite holiness directly and by ourselves

because of our sins; that we need Mary, His holy Mother, to be our advocate and Mediatrix with Him, our Mediator. It is to approach Jesus as our Mediator and Brother, and at the same time to humble ourselves before Him, as before our God and our Judge. In a word, it is to practice humility, which is always exceedingly pleasing to the heart of God.

IT PURIFIES AND EMBELLISHES OUR GOOD WORKS

37. To consecrate ourselves thus to Jesus through Mary is to place in Mary's hands our good actions, which although they may appear to us to be good, are often very imperfect and unworthy of the sight and the acceptance of God, before whom even the stars are not pure. Ah! Let us pray, then, to our dear Mother and Queen, that having received our poor present, she may purify it, sanctify it, embellish it and thus render it worthy of God. All that our soul possesses is of less value before God, the Heavenly Householder, when it comes to winning His friendship and favor, than a worm-eaten apple presented to the king by a poor farmer in payment of the rent of his farm. But what would such a farmer do if he were wise and if he were well liked by the queen? Would he not give his apple to the queen? And would she not out of kindness to the poor man, as also out of respect for the king, remove from the apple all that is worm-eaten or spoiled, and then place it in a gold dish and surround it with flowers? Would the king refuse to accept the apple then? Or would he not rather receive it with joy from the hands of the queen, who favors that poor man? "If you wish to present something to God, no matter how small it may be," says St. Bernard, "place it in Mary's hands, if you do not wish to be refused."

38. Great God, how insignificant everything that we do really is! But let us place all in Mary's hands by this devotion.

When we have given ourselves to Mary to the very utmost of our power, by despoiling ourselves completely in her honor, she will far outdo us in generosity and will repay us a hundredfold. She will communicate herself to us, with her merits and virtues; she will place our presents on the golden plate of her charity; she will clothe us, as Rebecca clothed Jacob, with the beautiful garments of her elder and only Son, Jesus Christ—that is, with His merits, which she has at her disposal; and thus, after we have despoiled ourselves of everything in her honor, we shall be "clothed in double garments"; that is, the garments, the ornaments, the perfumes, the merits and the virtues of Jesus and Mary clothe the soul of their slave, who has despoiled himself and who perseveres in his despoliation.[21]

CHARITY IN THE HIGHEST DEGREE

39. Moreover, to give ourselves thus to Our Lady is to practice charity towards our neighbor in the highest possible degree, because we give her all that we hold most dear and let her dispose of it at her will in favor of the living and the dead.

IT INCREASES THE GRACE OF GOD IN US

40. By this devotion we place our graces, merits and virtues in safety, for we make Mary the depository of them all, saying to her: "See, my dear Mother, here are the good works that I have been able to do through the grace of thy dear Son;

---

[21] This charming comment on the words of St. Bernard will console and encourage certain souls who grow weary and sad when they become conscious of their unworthiness and their insufficiency. As St. Louis De Montfort loves to say, and his saying is very true, Mary will be "their supplement" with God.

I am not able to keep them on account of my own weakness and inconstancy, and also because of the many wicked enemies who attack me day and night. Alas! One may see every day the cedars of Lebanon fall into the mire and the eagles, which had raised themselves to the sun, become birds of night; and so do a thousand of the just fall on my left hand and ten thousand on my right. But thou, my most powerful princess, sustain me lest I fall; keep all my possessions for fear I may be robbed of them. All I have I entrust to thee. I know well who thou art; therefore, I entrust myself entirely to thee; thou art faithful to God and to men; thou wilt not allow anything to perish that I entrust to thee; thou art powerful, and nothing can hurt thee nor rob thee of anything thou holdest in thy hands."[22] "When you follow Mary, you will not go astray; when you pray to her, you will not despair; when you think of her, you will not err; when she sustains you, you will not fall; when she protects you, you will not fear; when she leads you, you will not become tired; when she favors you, you will arrive safely."[23] And again: "She keeps her Son from striking us; she keeps the devil from hurting us; she keeps our virtues from escaping us; she keeps our merits from being destroyed; she keeps our graces from being lost." These are the words of St. Bernard. They express in substance all I have said. Were there but this one motive to incite in me a desire for this devotion—namely, that it is a sure means of keeping me in the grace of God and even of increasing that grace in me, my heart ought to burn with longing for it.

---

[22] These words ought to be considered by all who are concerned about their perseverance in grace and their interior perfection. Many there are who hesitate even to begin and many who draw back soon after starting, because they apprehend a possible failure or lack of perseverance.

[23] St. Bernard, *Inter flores,* cap. 135, *de Maria Virgine.*

IT RENDERS THE SOUL FREE

41. This devotion truly frees the soul with the liberty of the children of God. Since for love of Mary we reduce ourselves freely to slavery, she, out of gratitude, will dilate our heart, intensify our love and cause us to walk with giant steps in the way of God's commandments. She delivers the soul from weariness, sadness and scruples. It was this devotion which Our Lord taught to Mother Agnes of Jesus[24] as a sure means of delivering her from the severe sufferings and perplexities which troubled her. "Make thyself," He said, "My Mother's slave." She did so, and in a moment her troubles ceased.

OBEDIENCE TO THE COUNSELS OF THE CHURCH

42. To show that this devotion is rightfully authorized it would be necessary to mention the bulls of the Popes and the pastoral letters of the bishops, speaking in its favor; the indulgences granted to it; the confraternities established in its honor; the examples of the many Saints and illustrious persons who have practiced it. But all that I shall leave out.

---

[24] A Dominican nun who died in the odor of sanctity in the year 1634 at the convent of Langeac in Auvergne, France.

INTERIOR PRACTICE OF THE
HOLY SLAVERY OF LOVE

ITS GUIDING FORMULA

43. I have said that this devotion consists in doing all our actions with Mary, in Mary, through Mary and for Mary.

SCOPE OF THIS FORMULA

44. It is not enough to have given ourselves once as slaves to Jesus through Mary, nor is it enough to renew that act of consecration every month or every week. That alone would not make it a permanent devotion, nor could it bring the soul to that degree of perfection to which it is capable of raising it. It is not very difficult to enroll ourselves in a confraternity, nor to practice this devotion in as far as it prescribes a few vocal prayers every day; but the great difficulty is to enter into its spirit. Now its spirit consists in this, that we be interiorly dependent on Mary; that we be slaves of Mary, and through her, of Jesus.

I have found many people who, with admirable zeal, have adopted the exterior practices of this holy slavery of Jesus and Mary, but I have found only a few who have accepted its interior spirit, and still fewer who have persevered in it.

MEANING AND EXPLANATION OF THIS FORMULA

ACT *WITH* MARY

45. The essential practice of this devotion is to do all our actions *with* Mary. This means that we must take Our Lady as the perfect model of all that we do.

46. Before undertaking anything, we must renounce ourselves and our own views.[25] We must place ourselves as mere nothings before God, unable of ourselves to do anything that is supernaturally good or profitable to our salvation. We must have recourse to Our Lady, uniting ourselves to her and to her intentions, although they are not known to us; and through Mary we must unite ourselves to the intentions of Jesus Christ. In other words, we must place ourselves as instruments in the hands of Mary, that she may act in us and do with us and for us whatever she pleases, for the greater glory of her Son, and through the Son, for the glory of the Father; so that the whole work of our interior life and of our spiritual perfection is accomplished only by dependence on Mary.

---

[25] From these indications, however abstract, we may learn that the act of union with Mary, as understood by St. Louis be Montfort, requires two things in the work of our sanctification: 1) the removal of all obstacles by renouncing ourselves; 2) the union of our will with the will of God and of our actions with the impulse of Divine grace. Without that self-renunciation in all things, our union with Mary would be very imperfect, our dependence on her would be an illusion . Note also, that by telling us to renounce our own views and intentions, however good they be, in order to adopt those of Mary, De Montfort counsels the practice of that which is most perfect.

ACT *IN* MARY

47. We must do all things *in* Mary;[26] that is to say, we must become accustomed little by little to recollect ourselves interiorly and thus try to form within us some idea or spiritual image of Mary.[27] She will be, as it were, the oratory of our soul, in which we offer up all our prayers to God, without fear of not being heard; she will be to us a Tower of David, in which we take refuge from all our enemies; a burning lamp to enlighten our interior and to inflame us with Divine love; a sacred altar upon which we contemplate God in Mary and with her. In short, Mary will be the only means used by our soul in dealing with God; she will be our universal refuge. If we pray, we will pray in Mary; if we receive Jesus in Holy Communion, we will place Him in Mary, so that He may take His delight in her; if we do anything at all, we will act in Mary; everywhere and in all things we will renounce ourselves.

---

[26] In indicates an indwelling, an intimate union which produces unity. As St. Louis De Montfort expresses it, we must "enter into Mary's interior and stay there, adopting her views and feelings." Mary must become, as it were, the place and the atmosphere in which we live; her influence must penetrate us. As soon as this disposition of our soul has become habitual, we can say that we dwell in Mary, and having thus become as one moral person with her, we abide in her and she dwells in us, in the sense explained above.

[27] St. Teresa gives similar advice to beginners for keeping recollected and united with Our Lord when at prayer. She recommends the use of images, and in this she is of the same mind as St. Louis De Montfort, who had recourse to images and banners, to the erection of calvaries and of other exterior displays that appeal to the senses and elevate the soul to God.

ACT *THROUGH* MARY

48. We must never go to Our Lord except *through* Mary, through her intercession and her influence with Him. We must never be without

MARY WHEN WE PRAY TO JESUS.

ACT *FOR* MARY

49. 40 Lastly, we must do all our actions *for* Mary. This means that as slaves of this august princess, we must work only for her, for her interests and her glory—making this the immediate end of all our actions—and for the glory of God, which must be their final end. In everything we do, we must renounce our self-love, because very often self-love sets itself up in an imperceptible manner as the end of our actions. We should often repeat, from the bottom of our heart: "O my dear Mother! It is for thee that I go here or there; for thee that I do this or that; for thee that I suffer this pain or wrong."

PRACTICAL COUNSELS CONCERNING THE SPIRIT OF THE HOLY SLAVERY

NOT MORE PERFECT TO GO STRAIGHT TO JESUS WITH-OUT MARY

50. Beware, predestinate soul, of believing that it is more perfect to go straight to Jesus, straight to God. Without Mary, your action and your intention will be of little value; but if you go to God through Mary, your work will be

Mary's work, and consequently it will be sublime and most worthy of God.[28]

NOT NECESSARY TO FEEL AND ENJOY WHAT YOU SAY AND DO

51. Moreover, do not try to feel and enjoy what you say and do, but say and do everything with that pure faith which Mary had on earth and which she will communicate to you in due time. Poor little slave, leave to your Sovereign Queen the clear sight of God, the raptures, the joys, the satisfactions and the riches of Heaven, and content yourself with pure faith, although full of repugnance, distractions, weariness and dryness, and say: "Amen, so be it," to whatever Mary, your Mother, does in Heaven. That is the best you can do for the time being.[29]

---

[28] This does not mean that we may not approach Our Lord directly to speak to Him in prayer or contemplation; nor does it mean that in every action of ours we must think of Mary actually and distinctly; a virtual intention is sufficient. St. Louis De Montfort, indeed, says that our offering or act of consecration, if renewed but once a month or once a week , does not establish us in the spirit of this devotion, which is a state or a habit; yet he remarks that our interior look toward Mary, though it be but a general and hasty look, is sufficient to renew our offering.

[29] Useful advice to those who are but beginning and who might think that they do nothing good because they do not see or feel. St. Louis De Montfort reminds them of the truth that our union with God consists in an act of the will. In his *True Devotion* he says that that act may be either mental or expressed in words; it can be made in the twinkling of an eye. In his prayer to Mary , he makes us ask for detachment of the senses in our devotion.

NOT NECESSARY TO ENJOY IMMEDIATELY THE PRESENCE
OF MARY

52. Take great care also not to torment yourself should you
not enjoy immediately the sweet presence of the Blessed
Virgin in your soul, for this is a grace not given to all; and
even when God, out of His great mercy, has thus favored a
soul, it is always very easy to lose this grace, unless by frequent recollection the soul remains alive to that interior
presence of Mary. Should this misfortune befall you, return
calmly to your Sovereign Queen and make amends to her.[30]

WONDERFUL EFFECTS OF THIS INTERIOR PRACTICE

53. Experience will teach you much more about this devotion than I can tell you; and if you remain faithful to the
little I have taught you, you will find so many rich fruits of
grace in this practice that you will be surprised and filled
with joy.

54. Let us set to work then, dear soul, and by the faithful
practice of this devotion let us obtain the grace "that Mary's
soul may be in us to glorifY the Lord, that her spirit may be
in us to rejoice in God," as St. Ambrose says. "Do not think
that there was more glory and happiness in dwelling in
Abraham's bosom, which was called Paradise, than in the

---

[30] This interior presence of Mary is a favor St. Louis De Montfort
enjoyed in an exceptional degree, as we may see by reading his life.
He says: "It is a grace not given to all." Yet he exhorts us all to
practice his true devotion and promises to all without exception
"that Mary's soul will be in them." It is true, he always insists upon
the condition of perseverance in practicing this devotion. As there
are, however, but few souls who remain faithful to its spirit, even in
a lower degree, we must say that this presence of Mary is not given
to all.

bosom of Mary, in which God has placed His throne," as the learned Abbot Guerric says.

IT ESTABLISHES MARY'S LIFE IN THE SOUL

55. This devotion, faithfully practiced, produces many happy effects in the soul. The most important of them all is that it establishes, even here below, Mary's life in the soul, so that it is no longer the soul that lives, but Mary living in it; for Mary's life becomes its life. And when, by an unspeakable yet real grace, the Blessed Virgin is Queen in a soul, what wonders does she not work there! She is the worker of great wonders, particularly in our soul, but she works them in secret, in a way unknown to the soul itself, for were it to know, it might destroy the beauty of her works.

MARY CAUSES JESUS TO LIVE IN THAT SOUL

56. As Mary is the fruitful Virgin everywhere, she produces in the soul wherein she dwells purity of heart and body, purity of intention and of purpose, and fruitfulness in good works. Do not think, dear soul, that Mary, the most fruitful of all pure creatures, who has brought forth even a God, remains idle in a faithful soul. She will cause Jesus Christ to live in that soul, and the soul to live in constant union with Jesus Christ. "My dear children, with whom I am in labor again until Christ is formed in you." . If Jesus Christ is the fruit of Mary in each individual soul, as well as in all souls in general, He is, however, her fruit and her masterpiece more particularly in a soul in which she dwells.

MARY BECOMES EVERYTHING TO THAT SOUL

57. In fine, Mary becomes everything to that soul in the service of Jesus Christ. The mind will be enlightened by Mary's pure faith. The heart will be deepened by Mary's humility. It will be dilated and inflamed by Mary's charity; made clean by Mary's purity; noble and great by her motherly care. But why dwell any longer on this? Only experience can teach the wonders wrought by Mary, wonders so great that neither the wise nor the proud, nor even many of the devout can believe them.

SPECIAL FUNCTION OF THE HOLY SLAVERY

IN THE LATTER TIMES

THROUGH MARY, JESUS WILL REIGN

58. As it is through Mary that God came into the world the first time, in a state of humiliation and annihilation, may we not say that it is through Mary also that He will come the second time, as the whole Church expects Him to come, to rule everywhere and to judge the living and the dead? Who knows how and when that will be accomplished? I do know that God, Whose thoughts are as far removed from ours as Heaven is distant from the earth, will come in a time and a manner that men expect the least, even those who are most learned and most versed in Holy Scripture, which is very obscure on this subject.

59. We ought also to believe that toward the End of Time, and perhaps sooner than we think, God will raise up great men full of the Holy Ghost and imbued with the spirit of Mary, through whom this powerful Sovereign will work great

wonders in the world, so as to destroy sin and to establish the Kingdom of Jesus Christ, her Son, upon the ruins of the kingdom of this corrupt world; and these holy men will succeed by means of this devotion, of which I do but give here the outline and which my deficiency only impairs.

EXTERIOR PRACTICES OF THE
HOLY SLAVERY OF LOVE

60. Besides the interior practice of this devotion, of which we have just spoken, there are also certain exterior practices, which we must neither omit nor neglect.

CONSECRATION AND RENEWAL

61. The first one is to choose a special feast-day on which to consecrate ourselves to Jesus through the Blessed Virgin Mary, whose slaves we make ourselves. On the same day we should receive Holy Communion for that intention, and spend the day in prayer. At least once a year, on the same day, we should renew our act of consecration.

A TOKEN OF OUR SERVITUDE

62. The second one is to pay to Our Lady, every year on that same day, some little tribute, as a token of our servitude and dependence; such has always been the homage paid by slaves to their masters. That tribute may consist of an act of mortification, an alms, a pilgrimage or some prayers. Bl. Marino, we are told by his brother, St. Peter Damian, was wont to take the discipline in public every year on the same day before the altar of Our Lady. Such zeal is not required, nor

do we counsel it; but if we give but little to Mary, let us at least offer it with a humble and grateful heart.

CELEBRATION OF THE ANNUNCIATION

63. The third practice is to celebrate every year, with special devotion, the feast of the Annunciation, which is the patronal feast of this devotion and was established to honor and imitate the dependence in which the Eternal Word placed Himself on that day out of love for us.

RECITATION OF THE LITTLE CROWN AND THE MAGNIFICAT.

64. The fourth external practice is to say every day the Little Crown of the Blessed Virgin, which is composed of three Our Fathers and twelve Hail Marys; also, often to recite the Magnificat, which is the only hymn of Mary that we possess, to thank God for His graces in the past and to beg of Him fresh blessings for the present. Above all, we ought not to fail to say this hymn in thanksgiving after Holy Communion. The learned Gerson tells us that Our Lady herself was wont to recite it after Communion.

THE TREE OF LIFE: ITS CULTURE AND GROWTH

OR

HOW TO MAKE MARY LIVE
AND REIGN IN OUR SOULS

Predestinate soul, have you understood, by the grace of the Holy Ghost, what I have tried to explain to you in the preceding pages? If so, be thankful to God, for it is a secret known and understood by only a few. If you have found the treasure hidden in the field of Mary, the precious pearl of the Gospel, sell all that you have in order to buy it. You must make the sacrifice of yourself to the Blessed Mother, you must disappear in her, so that you may find God alone.

If the Holy Ghost has planted in your soul the true Tree of Life, which is the devotion that I have just explained to you, you must do all you can to cultivate it, in order that it may yield its fruit in due season. This devotion is like the mustard seed of the Gospel, "which is the least indeed of all seeds, but when it is grown up, is greater than all herbs, and becometh a tree, so that the birds of the air come and dwell in the branches thereof," and rest in its shade from the heat of the sun and hide there in safety from the beasts of prey.

This is the way, predestinate soul, to cultivate it:

NO HUMAN SUPPORT

This Tree, once planted in a faithful heart, requires the open air and freedom from all human support. Being Heavenly, it must be kept clear from any creatures that might prevent it from lifting itself to God, in Whom its origin lies. Hence, you must not rely on your own skill or your natural talents, on your own repute or the protection of men. You must have recourse to Mary and rely on her help alone.

CONSTANT CONCERN OF THE SOUL

The one in whose soul this Tree is planted must, like a good gardener, constantly watch over it and tend it, for it is a Tree that has life and is capable of yielding the fruit of life. Therefore, it must be cultivated and raised by the steady care and application of the soul; and the soul that would become perfect will make this its chief aim and occupation.

VIOLENCE TO ONESELF

Whatever is likely to choke the Tree or in the course of time prevent its yielding its fruit, such as thorns and thistles, must be cut away and rooted out. This means that by mortification and doing violence to ourselves, we must suppress and renounce all useless pleasures and vain traffic with creatures. In other words, we must crucify the flesh, keep recollected and mortify our senses.

NO SELF-LOVE

You must also keep watch on insects which might do harm to the Tree. These insects are self- love or love of comfort. They eat away the foliage of the Tree and destroy the fair hopes it gives of yielding fruit, for self-love is opposed to the love of Mary.

HORROR OF SIN

You must not allow destructive animals to approach the Tree of Life. By these animals are meant all sins. They may kill the Tree of Life by their touch alone. Even their breath must be kept away from it, namely, venial sins, for they are most dangerous if committed without regret.

FIDELITY TO RELIGIOUS PRACTICES

It is also necessary to water this Heavenly Tree often with the fervor of piety in our religious practices, in our Confessions and Communions, in all our prayers, both public and private; otherwise, it will stop yielding fruit.

PEACE IN TRIALS

Do not become alarmed when the Tree is moved and shaken by the wind, for it is necessary that the storms of temptation should threaten to uproot it, that snow and ice should cover it, so as, if possible, to destroy it. This means that this devotion will of necessity be attacked and contradicted, but provided we persevere in cultivating it in our souls, we need not fear.

ITS FRUIT: OUR LORD

Predestinate soul, if you thus cultivate the Tree of Life, freshly planted in your soul by the Holy Ghost, I assure you that in a short time it will grow so tall that the birds of Heaven will come to dwell in it. It will be a good tree, yielding fruit of honor and grace in due season, namely, the sweet and adorable Jesus, who always has been, and always will be, the only fruit of Mary.

Happy the soul in which Mary, the Tree of Life, is planted; happier the soul in which she has acquired growth and bloom; still happier the soul in which she yields her fruit; but most happy of all: the soul which relishes and preserves Mary's fruit until death, and for ever and ever. Amen.

"He who holdeth , let him hold ."

GOD ALONE

LITTLE CROWN OF THE BLESSED VIRGIN

St. John, the beloved disciple of Jesus and Mary, was privileged to behold a wonderful sign in Heaven: "A woman clothed with the sun, and the moon was under her feet, and upon her head a crown of twelve stars." This gave rise to the Crown of Twelve Stars devotion which Heaven has blessed with countless favors. St. John Berchmans made it his daily favorite.

This chaplet is prayed to honor each of those twelve stars as they symbolize her motherhood and queenship over all Israel, the twelve stars representing the 12 Tribes and the 12 Apostles. This devotion consists of 12 Aves—one for each star—broken up into 3 groups, each group representing an aspect of Mary's virtues: excellence, power, and goodness.

Each group begins with an Our Father, and ends with a Glory Be. The entire Crown, then, is the praying of the following arrangement of prayers three times:

1 Our Father 4 Hail Marys 1 Glory Be

Chaplet: On the medal:

Let us offer praise and thanksgiving to the Most Holy Trinity, Who hath shown us the Virgin Mary, clothed with the sun, the moon between her feet, and on her head a mystic crown of twelve stars.

R. For ever and ever. Amen.

On the first large bead:

Let us praise and thank the Divine Father, Who elected her for His daughter.

R. Amen. Say *Our Father.*

On the small bead:

Praised be the Divine Father, Who predestined her to be the Mother of His Divine Son.

R. Amen. Say *Hail Mary.*

On the small bead:

Praised be the Divine Father, Who preserved her from all stain in her conception.

R. Amen. Say *Hail Mary.*

On the small bead:

Praised be the Divine Father, Who adorned her at birth with His most excellent gifts.

R. Amen. Say *Hail Mary.*

On the small bead:

Praised be the Divine Father, Who gave her Saint Joseph to be her companion and most pure spouse.

R. Amen. Say *Hail Mary* and *Gloria.*

On the next large bead:

Let us praise and thank the Divine Son, Who chose her for His mother.

R. Amen. Say *Our Father.*

On the small bead:

Praised be the Divine Son, Who became incarnate in her bosom and there abode for nine months.

R. Amen. Say *Hail Mary.*

On the small bead:

Praised be the Divine Son, Who was born of her and was nourished at her breast.

R. Amen. Say *Hail Mary.*

On the small bead:

Praised be the Divine Son, Who in His childhood willed to be taught by her.

R. Amen. Say *Hail Mary.*

On the small bead:

Praised be the Divine Son, Who revealed to her the mystery of the Redemption of the world.

R. Amen. Say *Hail Mary* and *Gloria.*

On the next large bead:

Let us praise and thank the Holy Spirit, Who took her for His spouse.

R. Amen. Say *Our Father.*

On the small bead:

Praised be the Holy Spirit, Who, revealed first to her His Name of Holy Spirit.

R. Amen. Say *Hail Mary.*

On the small bead:

Praised be the Holy Spirit, by Whose operation she was at once Virgin and Mother.

R. Amen. Say *Hail Mary.*

On the small bead:

Praised be the Holy Spirit, by Whose power she was the living-temple of the ever-blessed Trinity.

R. Amen. Say *Hail Mary.*

On the small bead:

Praised be the Holy Spirit, by Whom she was exalted in Heaven above every living creature.

R. Amen. Say *Hail Mary* and *Gloria.*

Part III

THE CONFRATERNITY OF MARY, QUEEN OF ALL HEARTS

It is not necessary to join any religious group in order to make and live St. Louis De Montfort's Consecration to Jesus through Mary. However, those who so desire may join the Confraternity of Mary, Queen of All Hearts .

The Confraternity of Mary, Queen of All Hearts, was first established on March 25, 1899. Pope St. Pius X erected it as an Archconfraternity in Rome on April 28, 1913.

1. The "Confraternity of Mary Queen of All Hearts" has had its name changed to the "Association of Mary Queen of All Hearts," and at the same time has been combined with what used to be called the "Association of Priest of Mary, Queen of All Hearts." This was done by decree of the Congregation for Institutes of Religious Life and Societies of Apostolic Life on 26 April 2001.

Today there are eighty-eight branches of the Confraternity in various parts of the world: the United States, Canada, Haiti, South America, Europe, Asia and Africa. There are several hundred thousand members throughout the world.

OBJECT

The object of the Confraternity of Mary, Queen of All Hearts, is to establish within us the reign of Mary as a means of establishing more perfectly the reign of Jesus in our souls.

CONDITIONS OF MEMBERSHIP

One who, after the necessary formation and preparation, pronounces the consecration to Jesus, Eternal and Incarnate Wisdom, by the hands of Mary, according to the formula of Saint Louis-Marie de Montfort, may be received into the Association.

The incorporation is made, following the motivated request of the candidate and acceptance by the Director, at the moment when the consecration is made in the presence of the Director or his delegate and its inscription in the register of the Association.

COMMITMENTS

The consecration by which a person engages himself or herself in the Association implies the commitment to live, in one's own state of life, in one's own milieu, in one's own work, the spirit and the spirituality left us by Montfort. The members will seek to make it the heart of their lives, impregnating all their activities and apostolate.

Renewing their consecration each day, members collaborate, according to their possibilities and their own condition, in the apostolate of the Company of Mary following the directives of the Director General.

INDULGENCES

DECREE OF THE APOSTOLIC PENITENTIARY CONFIRMING INDULGENCES

PAENITENTIARIA APOSTOLICA

PROT. N. 65/01/I

HOLY FATHER

Ivo Libralato, Procurator General of the Montfortian Company of Mary, in the name of the Most Reverend Superior General of the same Congregation and as such Director of the Montfortian Associates of "Mary Queen of All Hearts," together with his Council, humbly petitions: Since the Congregation for Institutes of Religious Life and Societies of Apostolic Life, on 26 April last, duly recognised a new Statute for the former Associations, one clerical, the other lay, to be now reunited in one Association to be called the Association of "Mary, Queen of All Hearts," he requests that the grant of a Plenary Indulgence made by your Holiness, through a Rescript of the Apostolic Penitentiary, on 12 October 1996, granted in perpetuity, might be attributed to the new Association, by which the members might rejoice and receive the fruit of charity on days of piety, consecrating themselves to Christ through Mary, his most sweet Mother, according to the spirit and admirable example of Saint Louis Marie Grignion de Montfort.

The APOSTOLIC PENITENTIARY, at the behest of the Holy Father, rules that the members may acquire a Plenary Indulgence, provided that, the usual conditions (Sacramental Confession, Holy Communion and Prayer for the Holy Father's intentions) having been fulfilled and any attachment to any sin being excluded, they promise or renew their promise, at least privately, to faithfully observe their own Statutes, on the following occasions:

The day of their enrollment;

Holy Thursday;

The liturgical celebrations of Christmas and the Annunciation of the Lord;

The Immaculate Conception of the Blessed Virgin Mary and the feast of St. Louis Marie Grignion de Montfort;

And the first Saturday of every month.

The present rescript to be valid in perpetuity.

Anything to the contrary notwithstanding.

FEASTS OF THE CONFRATERNITY

The Annunciation, March 25, is the principal feast of the Confraternity, because that is the day on which Our Lord came to us through Mary and set us an example of complete dependence on her. The secondary feast is that of St. Louis De Montfort, April 28.

Other special feasts are the Immaculate Conception, Christmas, the Visitation, the Purification, the Assumption and the Feast of St. John the Evangelist, December 27.

Correspondence regarding the Confraternity should be sent to;

                          Rev. Father Director
                          The Confraternity
                          Montfort Fathers
                          26 South Saxon Ave.
                          Bay Shore, NY 11706

33-DAY PREPARATION FOR TOTAL CONSECRATION TO MARY

ST. LOUIS DE MONTFORT'S formula of total consecration to Jesus through Mary is not to be taken lightly. This is evidenced from the fact that the Saint himself advocates a serious preparation consisting of twelve preliminary days, in which the soul endeavours to rid itself of the spirit of the world as opposed to the spirit of Christ.

This is followed by three weeks of prayer and meditation during which the soul strives to acquire a better knowledge of self (First Week), of Mary (Second Week), and of Jesus Christ (Third Week). Though this preliminary period is strongly recommended, it is obvious that the length of time devoted to such a preparation may vary according to one's personal needs and circumstances.

This culminates in the final Act of Consecration to the Blessed Virgin that you may renew yearly or monthly, or even every day by giving all your actions to Mary. One of the most fruitful ways to carry out this consecration in your every-day life is to say the Holy Rosary every day.

INITIAL 12-DAY PREPARATION

EMPTYING YOURSELF OF THE
SPIRIT OF THE WORLD

EXAMINE your conscience, pray, practice renouncement of your own will; mortification, purity of heart. This purity is the indispensable condition for contemplating God in heaven, to see Him on earth and to know Him by the light of faith. The first part of the preparation should be employed in casting off the spirit of the world, which is contrary to that of Jesus Christ. The spirit of the world consists essentially in the denial of the supreme dominion of God; a denial which is manifested in practice by sin and disobedience; thus it is principally opposed to the spirit of Christ, which is also that of Mary.

It manifests itself by the concupiscence of the flesh, by the concupiscence of the eyes and by the pride of life, by disobedience to God's laws and the abuse of created things. Its works are: sin in all forms, then all else by which the devil leads to sin; works which bring error and darkness to the mind, and seduction and corruption to the will. Its pomp's are the splendour, and the charms employed by the devil to render sin alluring in persons, places and things.

DAY 1

Today's Reading: *Matthew 5:1–19*

And seeing the multitudes, he went up into a mountain, and when he was set down, his disciples came unto him. And opening his mouth, he taught them, saying: Blessed are the poor in spirit: for theirs is the kingdom of heaven. Blessed are the meek: for they shall possess the land. Blessed are they that mourn: for they shall be comforted. Blessed are they that hunger and thirst after justice: for they shall have their fill. Blessed are the merciful: for they shall obtain mercy. Blessed are the clean of heart: for they shall see God. Blessed are the peacemakers: for they shall be called children of God. Blessed are they that suffer persecution for justice' sake: for theirs is the kingdom of heaven. Blessed are ye when they shall revile you, and persecute you, and speak all that is evil against you, untruly, for my sake: Be glad and rejoice, for your reward is very great in heaven. For so they persecuted the prophets that were before you. You are the salt of the earth. But if the salt lose its savour, wherewith shall it be salted? It is good for nothing any more but to be cast out, and to be trodden on by men. You are the light of the world. A city seated on a mountain cannot be hid. Neither do men light a candle and put it under a bushel, but upon a candlestick, that it may shine to all that are in the house. So let your light shine before men, that they may see your good works, and glorify your Father who is in heaven. Do not think that I am come to destroy the law, or the prophets. I am not come to destroy, but to fulfill. For amen I say unto you, till heaven and earth pass, one jot, or one tittle shall not pass of the law, till all be fulfilled. He therefore that shall break one of these least commandments, and shall so teach men, shall be called the least in the kingdom of heaven. But he that shall do and teach, he shall be called great in the kingdom of heaven.

PRAYERS

Veni Creator Spiritus
Ave Maris Stella
Magnificat
Glory Be

DAY 2

Today's Reading: *Matthew 5:48, 6:1–15*

Be you therefore perfect, as also your heavenly Father is perfect. . . . Take heed that you do not your justice before men, to be seen by them: otherwise you shall not have a reward of your Father who is in heaven. Therefore when thou dost an almsdeed, sound not a trumpet before thee, as the hypocrites do in the synagogues and in the streets, that they may be honoured by men. Amen I say to you, they have received their reward. But when thou dost alms, let not thy left hand know what thy right hand doth. That thy alms may be in secret, and thy Father who seeth in secret will repay thee. And when ye pray, you shall not be as the hypocrites, that love to stand and pray in the synagogues and corners of the streets, that they may be seen by men: Amen I say to you, they have received their reward. But thou when thou shalt pray, enter into thy chamber, and having shut the door, pray to thy Father in secret: and thy Father who seeth in secret will repay thee. And when you are praying, speak not much, as the heathens. For they think that in their much speaking they may be heard. Be not you therefore like to them, for your Father knoweth what is needful for you, before you ask him. Thus therefore shall you pray: Our Father who art in heaven, hallowed be thy name. Thy kingdom come. Thy will be done on earth as it is in heaven. Give us this day our supersubstantial bread. And forgive us our debts, as we also forgive our debtors. And lead us not into temptation. But deliver us from evil. Amen. For if you will forgive men their offences, your heavenly Father will forgive you also your offences. But if you will not forgive men, neither will your Father forgive you your offences.

PRAYERS

Veni Creator Spiritus
Ave Maris Stella
Magnificat
Glory Be

DAY 3

Today's Reading: *Matthew 7:1–14*

Judge not, that you may not be judged, For with what judgment you judge, you shall be judged: and with what measure you mete, it shall be measured to you again. Any why seest thou the mote that is in thy brother's eye; and seest not the beam that is in thy own eye? Or how sayest thou to thy brother: Let me cast the mote out of thy eye; and behold a beam is in thy own eye? Thou hypocrite, cast out first the beam in thy own eye, and then shalt thou see to cast out the mote out of thy brother's eye. Give not that which is holy to dogs; neither cast ye your pearls before swine, lest perhaps they trample them under their feet, and turning upon you, they tear you. Ask, and it shall be given you: seek, and you shall find: knock, and it shall be opened to you. For every one that asketh, receiveth: and he that seeketh, findeth: and to him that knocketh, it shall be opened. Or what man is there among you, of whom if his son shall ask bread, will he reach him a stone? Or if he shall ask him a fish, will he reach him a serpent? If you then being evil, know how to give good gifts to your children: how much more will your Father who is in heaven, give good things to them that ask him? All things therefore whatsoever you would that men should do to you, do you also to them. For this is the law and the prophets. Enter ye in at the narrow gate: for wide is the gate, and broad is the way that leadeth to destruction, and many there are who go in thereat. How narrow is the gate, and strait is the way that leadeth to life: and few there are that find it!

PRAYERS

Veni Creator Spiritus
Ave Maris Stella
Magnificat
Glory Be

DAY 4

Today's Reading: *Imitation of Christ: Book 3, Chapters 7, 40*

That man has no good of himself, and that he cannot glory in anything Lord, what is man, that Thou art mindful of him; or the son of man, that Thou visit him? What has man deserved that Thou should give him grace? Lord, what cause have I to complain, if Thou forsakest me, or what can I justly allege, if what I petition Thou shalt not grant? This most assuredly, I may truly think and say: Lord I am nothing, I can do nothing of myself, that is good, but I am in all things defective and ever tend to nothing. And unless I am assisted and interiorly instructed by Thee, I become wholly tepid and relaxed, but Thou, O Lord, art always the same, and endurest unto eternity, ever good, just and holy, doing all things well, justly and holily and disposing them in wisdom.

But I who am more inclined to go back, than to go forward, continue not always in one state, for I am changed, seven different times. But it quickly becomes better when it pleases Thee, and Thou stretchest out Thy helping hand: for Thou alone, without man's aid can assist me and so strengthen me, that my countenance shall be more diversely changed: but my heart be converted and find its rest in Thee alone.

He who would be too secure in time of peace will often be found too much dejected in time of war. If you could always continue to be humble and little in your own eyes, and keep your spirit in due order and subjection, you would not fall so easily into danger and offense. It is good counsel that, when you have conceived the spirit of fervor, you should meditate how it will be when that light shall be withdrawn.

PRAYERS

Veni Creator Spiritus
Ave Maris Stella
Magnificat
Glory Be

DAY 5

Today's Reading: *Imitation of Christ: Book 3, Chapter 40*

Wherefore, but I did know well, how to cast from me all human comfort, either for the sake of devotion, or through the necessity by which I am compelled to seek Thee, because there is no man that can comfort me. Then might I deservedly hope in Thy favor, and rejoice in the gift of a new consolation. Thanks be to Thee from Whom all things proceed, as often as it happens to me. I, indeed, am but vanity, and nothing in Thy sight , an inconstant and weak man. Where, therefore, can I glory, or for what do I desire to be thought of highly?

Forsooth of my very nothingness; and this is most vain. Truly vainglory is an evil plague, because it draws away from true glory, and robs us of heavenly grace. For, while a man takes complacency in himself, he displeases Thee; while he wants for human applause, he is deprived of true virtues. But true, glory and holy exultation is to glory in Thee, and not in one's self; to rejoice in Thy Name, but not in one's own strength. To find pleasure in no creature, save only for Thy sake. Let Thy Name be praised, not mine; let Thy work be magnified, not mine; let Thy Holy Name be blessed, but let nothing be attributed to me of the praise of men. Thou art my glory; Thou art the exultation of my heart; in Thee, will I glory and rejoice all the day; but for myself, I will glory in nothing but in my infirmities.

PRAYERS

Veni Creator Spiritus
Ave Maris Stella
Magnificat
Glory Be

DAY 6

Today's Reading: *Imitation of Christ: Book 1, Chapter 18*

On the Example of the Holy Fathers

Look upon the lively examples of the holy Fathers in whom shone real perfection and the religious life, and you will see how little it is, and almost nothing that we do. Alas, what is our life when we compare it with theirs? Saints and friends of Christ, they served our Lord in hunger and in thirst, in cold, in nakedness, in labor and in weariness, in watching, in fasting, prayers and holy meditations, and in frequent persecutions and reproaches. Oh, how many grievous tribulations did the Apostles suffer and the Martyrs and Confessors and Virgins, and all the rest who resolved to follow the steps of Christ! For they hated their lives in this world, that they might keep them in life everlasting. Oh what a strict and self-renouncing life the holy Fathers of the desert led! What long and grievous temptations did they bear! How often were they harassed by the enemy, what frequent and fervent prayers did they offer up to God, what rigorous abstinence did they practice!

What a valiant contest waged they to subdue their imperfections! What purity and straightforwardness of purpose kept they towards God! By day they laboured, and much of the night they spent in prayer; though while they laboured, they were far from leaving off mental prayer. They spent all their time profitably. Every hour seemed short to spend with God; and even their necessary bodily refreshment was forgotten in the great sweetness of contemplation. They renounced all riches, dignities, honours and kindred; they hardly took what was necessary for life. It grieved them to serve the body even in its necessity. Accordingly, they were poor in earthly things, but very rich in grace and virtues.

PRAYERS

Veni Creator Spiritus
Ave Maris Stella
Magnificat
Glory Be

DAY 7

Today's Reading: *Imitation of Christ: Book 1, Chapter 18 (continued)*

Outwardly they suffered want, but within they were re-freshed with grace and Divine consolation. They were aliens to the world; they seemed as nothing and the world despised them; but they were precious and beloved in the sight of God. They persevered in true humility, they lived in simple obedience, they walked in charity and patience, and so every day they advanced in spirit and gained great favour with God. They were given for example to all religious, and ought more to excite us to advance in good, than the number of lukewarm to induce us to grow remiss. Oh! how great was the fervour of all religious in the beginning of their holy institute! Oh, how great was their devotion in prayer, how great was their zeal for virtue! How vigorous the discipline that was kept up, what reverence and obedience, under the rule of the superior, flourished in all! Their traces that remain still bear witness, that they were truly holy and perfect men who did battle so stoutly, and trampled the world under their feet. Now, he is thought great who is not a transgressor; and who can, with patience, endure what he has undertaken. Ah, the lukewarm and negligence of our state! That we soon fall away from our first fervour, and are even now tired with life, from slothfulness and tepidity. Oh that advancement in virtue be not quite asleep in thee, who has so often seen the manifold examples of the devout!

PRAYERS

Veni Creator Spiritus
Ave Maris Stella
Magnificat
Glory Be

DAY 8

Today's Reading: *Imitation of Christ: Book 1, Chapter 18*

Of Resisting Temptations

As long as we live in this world, we cannot be without temptations and tribulations. Hence it is written in Job "Man's life on earth is a temptation." Everyone therefore should be solicitous about his temptations and watch in prayer lest the devil find an opportunity to catch him: who never sleeps, but goes about, seeking whom he can devour. No one is so perfect and holy as sometimes not to have temptations and we can never be wholly free from them. Nevertheless, temptations are very profitable to man, troublesome and grievous though they may be, for in them, a man is humbled, purified and instructed. All the Saints passed through many tribulations and temptations and were purified by them. And they that could not support temptations, became reprobate, and fell away.

Many seek to flee temptations, and fall worse into them. We cannot conquer by flight alone, but by patience and true humility we become stronger than all our enemies. He who only declines them outwardly, and does not pluck out their root, will profit little; nay, temptations will sooner return and he will find himself in a worse condition. By degrees and by patience you will, by God's grace, better overcome them than by harshness and your own importunity. Take council the oftener in temptation, and do not deal harshly with one who is tempted; but pour in consolation, as thou wouldst wish to be done unto yourself. Inconstancy of mind and little confidence in God, is the beginning of all temptations. For as a ship without a helm is driven to and fro by the waves, so the man who neglects and gives up his resolutions is tempted in many ways.

PRAYERS

Veni Creator Spiritus
Ave Maris Stella
Magnificat
Glory Be

DAY 9

Today's Reading: *Imitation of Christ: Book 1, Chapter 13 (continued)*

Fire tries iron, and temptation a just man. We often know not what we are able to do, but temptations discover what we are. Still, we must watch, especially in the beginning of temptation; for then the enemy is more easily overcome, if he be not suffered to enter the door of the mind, but is withstood upon the threshold the very moment he knocks. Whence a certain one has said "Resist beginnings; all too late the cure." When ills have gathered strength, by long delay, first there comes from the mind a simple thought; then a strong imagination, afterwards delight, and the evil motion and consent and so, little by little the fiend does gain entrance, when he is not resisted in the beginning. The longer anyone has been slothful in resisting, so much the weaker he becomes, daily in himself, and the enemy, so much the stronger in him. Some suffer grievous temptations in the beginning of their conversion, others in the end and others are troubled nearly their whole life. Some are very lightly tempted, according to the wisdom and the equity of the ordinance of God who weighs man's condition and merits, and pre-ordaineth all things for the salvation of His elect. We must not, therefore, despair when we are tempted, but the more fervently pray to God to help us in every tribulation: Who, of a truth, according to the sayings of St. Paul, will make such issue with the temptation, that we are able to sustain it.

Let us then humble our souls under the hand of God in every temptation and tribulation, for the humble in spirit, He will save and exalt. In temptation and tribulations, it is proved what progress man has made; and there also is great merit, and virtue is made more manifest.

PRAYERS

Veni Creator Spiritus
Ave Maris Stella
Magnificat
Glory Be

DAY 10

Today's Reading: *Imitation of Christ: Book 3, Chapter 10*

That it is sweet to despise the world and to serve God

King Who is on high: Oh, how great is the abundance of Thy sweetness, O Lord, which Thou hast hidden for those that fear Thee! But what art Thou, for those who love Thee? What, to those who serve Thee with their whole heart? Unspeakable indeed is the sweetness of Thy contemplation, which Thou bestowest on those who love Thee. In this most of all hast Thou showed me the sweetness of Thy love, that when I had no being, Thou didst make me; and when I was straying far from Thee, Thou brought me back again, that I might serve Thee: and Thou hast commanded me to serve Thee. O Fountain of everlasting love, what shall I say of Thee? How can I forget Thee, Who hast vouchsafed to remember me even after I was corrupted and lost? Beyond all hope Thou showest mercy to Thy servant; and beyond all desert, hast Thou manifested Thy grace and friendship. What return shall I make to Thee for this favour? For it is granted to all who forsake these things, to renounce the world, and to assume the monastic life. Is it much that I should serve Thee, Whom the whole creation is bound to serve? It ought not to seem much to me to serve Thee; but this does rather appear great and wonderful to me, that Thou vouch safest to receive one so wretched and unworthy as Thy servant. It is a great honor, a great glory, to serve Thee, and to despise all things for Thee, for they who willingly subject themselves to Thy holy service, shall have great grace. They shall experience the sweetest consolation of the Holy Spirit, Who for the love of Thee, have cast aside all carnal delight.

PRAYERS

Veni Creator Spiritus
Ave Maris Stella
Magnificat
Glory Be

DAY 11

Today's Reading: *Imitation of Christ: Book 1, Chapter 25*

On the Fervent Amendment of our Whole Life

When a certain anxious person, who often times wavered between hope and fear, once overcome with sadness, threw himself upon the ground in prayer, before one of the altars in the Church and thinking these things in his mind, said "Oh, if I only knew how to persevere," that very instant he heard within him, this heavenly answer: "And if thou didst know this, what would thou do? Do now what you would do, and thou shall be perfectly secure." And immediately being consoled, and comforted, he committed himself to the Divine Will, and his anxious thoughts ceased. He no longer wished for curious things; searching to find out what would happen to him, but studied rather to learn what was the acceptable and perfect will of God for the beginning and the perfection of every good work.

"Hope in the Lord," said the Prophet, "And do all good, and inhabit the land, and thou shall be fed of the riches thereof."

There is one thing that keeps many back from spiritual progress, and from fervor in amendment namely: the labor that is necessary for the struggle. And assuredly they especially advance beyond others in virtues, who strive the most manfully to overcome the very things which are the hardest and most contrary to them. For there a man does profit more and merit more abundant grace, when he does most to overcome himself and mortify his spirit. All have not, indeed, equal difficulties to overcome and mortify, but a diligent and zealous person will make a greater progress though he have more passions than another, who is well regulated but less fervent in the pursuit of virtues.

PRAYERS

Veni Creator Spiritus
Ave Maris Stella
Magnificat
Glory Be

DAY 12

Today's Reading: *Imitation of Christ: Book 1, Chapter 25 (continued)*

But if thou observest anything worthy of reproof, beware thou do not the same. And if at any time thou hast done it, labour quickly to amend thyself. As thine eye observeth others, so art thou by others noted again?

How sweet and pleasant a thing it is, to see brethren fervent and devout, obedient and well-disciplined! How sad and

grievous a thing it is, to see them walk disorderly, not apply-
ing themselves to that for which they are called! How hurtful
a thing it is, when they neglect the purpose of their calling
and busy themselves in things not committed to their care!

Be mindful of the purpose thou hast embraced, and set
always before thee the image of the Crucified. Good cause
thou hast to be ashamed in looking upon the life of Jesus
Christ, seeing thou hast not as yet endeavoured to conform
thyself more unto Him, though thou hast been a long time
in the way of God. A religious person that exerciseth himself
seriously and devoutly in the most holy life and passion of
our Lord, shall there abundantly find whatsoever is profitable
and necessary for him, neither shall he need to seek any
better thing, besides Jesus. O if Jesus crucified would come
into our hearts, how quickly and fully should we be. A man
fervent and diligent is prepared for all things.

It is harder toil to resist vices and passions, than to sweat in
bodily labours. He that avoideth not small faults, by little
and little falleth into greater. Thou wilt always rejoice in the
evening, if thou spend the day profitably. Be watchful over
thyself, stir up thyself, warn thyself, and whatsoever becometh of others, neglect not thyself. The more violent thou
uses against thyself, the more shalt thou progress. Amen.

PRAYERS

Veni Creator Spiritus
Ave Maris Stella
Magnificat
Glory Be

WEEK ONE

OBTAIN KNOWLEDGE OF YOURSELF

PRAYERS, examinations, reflection, acts of renouncement of our own will, of contrition for our sins, of contempt of self, all performed at the feet of Mary, for it is from her that we hope for light to know ourselves. It is near her, we shall be able to measure the abyss of our miseries without despairing.

We should employ all our pious actions in asking for knowledge of ourselves and contrition of our sins: and we should do this in a spirit of piety. During this period, we shall consider not so much the opposition that exists between the spirit of Jesus and ours, as the miserable and humiliating state to which our sins have reduced us. Moreover, the True Devotion being an easy, short, sure and perfect way to arrive at that union with Our Lord which is Christ like perfection, we shall enter seriously upon this way, strongly convinced of our misery and helplessness. But how attain this without knowledge of ourselves'?

DAY 13

Today's Reading: *Luke 11:1–10*

And it came to pass, that as he was in a certain place praying, when he ceased, one of his disciples said to him: Lord, teach us to pray, as John also taught his disciples. And he said to them: When you pray, say: Father, hallowed be thy name. Thy kingdom come. Give us this day our daily bread. And forgive us our sins, for we also forgive every one that is indebted to us. And lead us not into temptation.

And he said to them: Which of you shall have a friend, and shall go to him at midnight, and shall say to him: Friend, lend me three loaves, because a friend of mine is come off his journey to me, and I have not what to set before him. And he from within should answer, and say: Trouble me not, the door is now shut, and my children are with me in bed; I cannot rise and give thee. Yet if he shall continue knocking, I say to you, although he will not rise and give him, because he is his friend; yet, because of his importunity, he will rise, and give him as many as he needeth.

And I say to you, Ask, and it shall be given you: seek, and you shall find: knock and it shall be opened to you. For every one that asketh, receiveth; and he that seeketh, findeth; and to him that knocketh, it shall be opened.

PRAYERS

Litany of the Holy Ghost
Litany of the Blessed Virgin Mary (Litany of Loreto)

Ave Maris Stella

DAY 14

Today's Reading: *Imitation of Christ: Book 3, Chapter 13*

*Of the Obedience of One in Humble Subjection, After the
Example of Jesus Christ*

My son, he that endeavoreth to withdraw himself from
obedience, withdraweth himself from grace; and he who
seeketh for himself private benefit (Matt. 16:24), loseth those
which are common. He that doth not cheerfully and freely
submit himself to his superior, it is a sign that his flesh is not
as yet perfectly obedient unto him, but oftentimes kicketh
and murmureth against him. Learn thou therefore quickly to
submit thyself to thy superior, if thou desire to keep thine
own flesh under the yoke. For more speedily is the outward
enemy overcome, if the inward man be not laid waste. There
is neither worse nor more troublesome enemy to the soul
than thou art unto thyself, if thou be not well in harmony
with the Spirit. It is altogether necessary that thou take up a
true contempt for thyself, if thou desire to prevail against
flesh and blood. Because as yet thou lovest thyself too inor-
dinately, therefore thou art afraid to resign thyself wholly to
the will of others. And yet, what great matter is it, if thou,
who art but dust and nothing, subject thyself to a man for
God's sake, when I, the Almighty and the Most Highest who
created all things of nothing, humbly subjected Myself to
man for thy sake?

I became of all men the most humble and the most abject
(Luke 2:7; John 13:14), that thou mightest overcome thy

pride with My humility. O dust! Learn to be obedient. Learn to humble thyself, thou earth and clay, and to bow thyself down under the feet of all men. Learn to break thine own wishes, and to yield thyself to all subjection.

PRAYERS

Litany of the Holy Ghost
Litany of the Blessed Virgin Mary (Litany of Loreto)
Ave Maris Stella

DAY 15

Today's Reading: *Luke 13:1–5*

Examples Inviting Repentance

And there were present, at that very time, some that told him of the Galileans, whose blood Pilate had mingled with their sacrifices. And he answering, said to them: Think you that these Galileans were sinners above all the men of Galilee, because they suffered such things? No, I say to you: but unless you shall do penance, you shall all likewise perish. Or those eighteen upon whom the tower fell in Siloe, and slew them: think you, that they also were debtors above all the men that dwelt in Jerusalem? No, I say to you; but except you do penance, you shall all likewise perish.

THE SECRET OF MARY

True Devotion to the Blessed Virgin Mary, Nos. 81 and 82

We Need Mary in order to Die to Ourselves

Secondly, in order to empty ourselves of self, we must die daily to ourselves. This involves our renouncing what the powers of the soul and the senses of the body incline us to do. We must see as if we did not see, hear as if we did not hear and use the things of this world as if we did not use them. This is what St. Paul calls "dying daily." Unless the grain of wheat falls to the ground and dies, it remains only a single grain and does not bear any good fruit. If we do not die to self and if our holiest devotions do not lead us to this necessary and fruitful death, we shall not bear fruit of any worth and our devotions will cease to be profitable. All our good works will be tainted by self-love and self-will so that our greatest sacrifices and our best actions will be unacceptable to God. Consequently when we come to die we shall find ourselves devoid of virtue and merit and discover that we do not possess even one spark of that pure love which God shares only with those who have died to themselves and whose life is hidden with Jesus Christ in him.

Thirdly, we must choose among all the devotions to the Blessed Virgin the one which will lead us more surely to this dying to self. This devotion will be the best and the most sanctifying for us.

PRAYERS

Litany of the Holy Ghost
Litany of the Blessed Virgin Mary (Litany of Loreto)
Ave Maris Stella

DAY 16

Today's Reading: *True Devotion to the Blessed Virgin Mary,*
No. 228

Preparatory Exercises

During the first week they should offer up all their prayers
and acts of devotion to acquire knowledge of themselves and
sorrow for their sins. Let them perform all their actions in a
spirit of humility. With this end in view they may, if they
wish, meditate on what I have said concerning our corrupted
nature, and consider themselves during six days of the week
as nothing but sails, slugs, toads, swine, snakes and goats. Or
else they may meditate on the following three considerations
of St. Bernard: "Remember what you were -corrupted seed;
what you are—a body destined for decay; what you will be -
food for worms." They will ask our Lord and the Holy Spirit
to enlighten them saying, "Lord, that I may see," or "Lord,
let me know myself," or the "Come, Holy Spirit." Every day
they should say the Litany of the Holy Spirit, with the prayer
that follows, as indicated in the first part of this work. They
will turn to our Blessed Lady and beg her to obtain for them
that great grace which is the foundation of all others, the
grace of self-knowledge. For this intention they will say each
day the Ave Maris Stella and the Litany of the Blessed Virgin.

Imitation of Christ: Book 2, Chapter 5

Of Self-consideration

We cannot trust over much to ourselves (Jer. 17:5), because grace oftentimes is wanting to us, and understanding also. Little light is there in us, and this we quickly lose by our negligence. Oftentimes too we perceive not our inward blindness how great it is. Oftentimes we do evil, and excuse it worse (Psalm 141:4). We are sometimes moved with passion, and we think it zeal. We reprehend small things in others, and pass over our own greater matters (Matt. 7:5). Quickly enough we feel and weigh what we suffer at the hands of others; but we mind not how much others suffer from us. He that well and rightly considereth his own works, will find little cause to judge hardly of another.

PRAYERS

Litany of the Holy Ghost
Litany of the Blessed Virgin Mary (Litany of Loreto)
Ave Maris Stella

DAY 17

Today's Reading: *Imitation of Christ: Book 1, Chapter 24*

Of Judgment, and the Punishment of Sinners

In all things look to the end; and how thou wilt stand before that strict Judge (Heb. 10:31) to whom nothing is hid, who is not appeased with gifts, nor admitteth excuses, but will judge according to right. O wretched and foolish sinner, who sometimes art in terror at the countenance of an angry man, what answer wilt thou make to God who knoweth all thy wickedness (Job 9:2)! Why dost thou not provide for thyself (Luke 16:9) against the day of judgement, when no man can be excused of defended by another, but everyone shall be a sufficient burden for himself!

Luke 16:1–8

The Crafty Steward

And he said also to his disciples: There was a certain rich man who had a steward: and the same was accused unto him, that he had wasted his goods. And he called him, and said to him: How is it that I hear this of thee? Give an account of thy stewardship: for now thou canst be steward no longer. And the steward said within himself: What shall I do, because my lord taketh away from me the stewardship? To dig I am not able; to beg I am ashamed. I know what I will do, that when I shall be removed from the stewardship, they may receive me into their houses. Therefore calling together every one of his lord's debtors, he said to the first: How much dost thou owe my lord? But he said: An hundred barrels of oil. And he said to him: Take thy bill and sit down quickly, and write fifty. Then he said to another: And how much dost thou owe? Who said: An hundred quarters of wheat? He said to him: Take thy bill, and write eighty. And the lord commended the unjust steward, forasmuch as he had done wisely: for the children of this world are wiser in their generation than the children of light.

PRAYERS

Litany of the Holy Ghost

Litany of the Blessed Virgin Mary (Litany of Loreto)
Ave Maris Stella

DAY 18

Today's Reading: *Luke 17:1–10*

On Leading Others Astray

And he said to his disciples: It is impossible that scandals should not come: but woe to him through whom they come. It were better for him, that a millstone were hanged about his neck, and he cast into the sea, than that he should scandalize one of these little ones.

On Brotherly Correction

Take heed to yourselves. If thy brother sin against thee, reprove him: and if he do penance, forgive him. And if he sin against thee seven times in a day, and seven times in a day be converted unto thee, saying, I repent; forgive him.

The Power of Faith

And the apostles said to the Lord: Increase our faith. And the Lord said: If you had faith like to a grain of mustard seed, you might say to this mulberry tree, Be thou rooted up, and be thou transplanted into the sea: and it would obey you.

Humble Service

But which of you having a servant ploughing, or feeding cattle, will say to him, when he is come from the field: Immediately go, sit down to meat: And will not rather say to him: Make ready my supper, and gird thyself, and serve me, whilst I eat and drink, and afterwards thou shalt eat and drink? Doth he thank that servant, for doing the things which he commanded him? I think not. So you also, when you shall have done all these things that are commanded you, say: We are unprofitable servants; we have done that which we ought to do.

Imitation of Christ: Book 3, Chapter 47

That All Grievous Things Are to Be Endured For the Sake of Eternal Life

My son, be not wearied out by the labours which thou hast undertaken for My sake, nor let tribulation cast thee down ever at all; but let My promise strengthen and comfort thee under every circumstance. I am well able to reward thee, above all measure and degree. Thou shalt not long toil here, nor always be oppressed with grief's. Wait a little while, and thou shalt see a speedy end of thine evils.

PRAYERS

Litany of the Holy Ghost
Litany of the Blessed Virgin Mary (Litany of Loreto)
Ave Maris Stella

DAY 19

Today's Reading: *Luke 18:15–30*

Jesus and the Children

And they brought unto him also infants, that he might touch them. Which when the disciples saw, they rebuked them. But Jesus, calling them together, said: Suffer children to come to me, and forbid them not: for of such is the kingdom of God. Amen, I say to you: Whosoever shall not receive the kingdom of God as a child, shall not enter into it.

The Rich Aristocrat

And a certain ruler asked him, saying: Good master, what shall I do to possess everlasting life? And Jesus said to him: Why dost thou call me good? None is good but God alone. Thou knowest the commandments: Thou shalt not kill: Thou shalt not commit adultery: Thou shalt not steal: Thou shalt not bear false witness: Honour thy father and mother. Who said: All these things have I kept from my youth. Which when Jesus had heard, he said to him: Yet one thing is wanting to thee: sell all whatever thou hast, and give to the poor, and thou shalt have treasure in heaven: and come, follow me. He having heard these things, became sorrowful; for he was very rich.

The Danger of Riches

And Jesus seeing him become sorrowful, said: How hardly shall they that have riches enter into the kingdom of God. For it is easier for a camel to pass through the eye of a needle, than for a rich man to enter into the kingdom of God. And they that heard it, said: Who then can be saved? He said to them: The things that are impossible with men, are possible with God.

The Reward of Renunciation

Then Peter said: Behold, we have left all things, and have followed thee. Who said to them: Amen, I say to you, there is no man that hath left house, or parents, or brethren, or wife, or children, for the kingdom of God's sake, Who shall not receive much more in this present time, and in the world to come life everlasting.

PRAYERS

Litany of the Holy Ghost
Litany of the Blessed Virgin Mary (Litany of Loreto)
Ave Maris Stella

WEEK TWO

OBTAIN KNOWLEDGE OF THE BLESSED VIRGIN

ACTS OF LOVE, pious affection for the Blessed Virgin, imitation of her virtues, especially her profound humility, her lively faith, her blind obedience, her continual mental prayer, her mortification in all things, her surpassing purity, her ardent charity, her heroic patience, her angelic sweetness, and her divine wisdom: "there being," as St. Louis De Montfort says, "the ten principal virtues of the Blessed Virgin."

We must unite ourselves to Jesus through Mary—this is the characteristic of our devotion; therefore, Saint Louis De Montfort asks that we employ ourselves in acquiring knowledge of the Blessed Virgin.

Mary is our sovereign and our mediator our Mother and our Mistress. Let us then endeavour to know the effects of this royalty, of this mediation, and of this maternity, as well as the grandeurs and prerogatives, which are the foundation or consequences thereof. Our Mother is also a perfect mould wherein we are to be moulded in order to make her intentions and dispositions ours. This we cannot achieve without studying the interior life of Mary; namely, her virtues, her sentiments, her actions, her participation in the mysteries of Christ, and her union with Him.

DAY 20

Today's Reading: Luke 2:16–21, 45–52

And they came with haste; and they found Mary and Joseph, and the infant lying in the manger. And seeing, they understood of the word that had been spoken to them concerning this child. And all that heard, wondered; and at those things that were told them by the shepherds. But Mary kept all these words, pondering them in her heart. And the shepherds returned, glorifying and praising God, for all the things they had heard and seen, as it was told unto them. And after eight days were accomplished, that the child should be circumcised, his name was called JESUS, which was called by the angel, before he was conceived in the womb. . . .

And not finding him, they returned into Jerusalem, seeking him. And it came to pass, that, after three days, they found him in the temple, sitting in the midst of the doctors, hearing them, and asking them questions. And all that heard him were astonished at his wisdom and his answers. And seeing him, they wondered. And his mother said to him: Son, why hast thou done so to us? behold thy father and I have sought thee sorrowing. And he said to them: How is it that you sought me? did you not know, that I must be about my father's business? And they understood not the word that he spoke unto them. And he went down with them, and came to Nazareth, and was subject to them. And his mother kept all these words in her heart. And Jesus advanced in wisdom, and age, and grace with God and men.

PRAYERS

Litany of the Holy Ghost
Litany of the Blessed Virgin Mary (Litany of Loreto)
Ave Maris Stella
St. Louis De Montfort's Prayer to Mary
Pray the Rosary

DAY 21

Today's Reading: *The Secret of Mary: Nos. 23–24*

True Devotion to Our Blessed Lady

If we would go up to God, and be united with Him, we must use the same means He used to come down to us to be made Man and to impart His graces to us. This means is a true devotion to our Blessed Lady. There are several true devotions to our Lady: here I do not speak of those which are false. The first consists in fulfilling our Christian duties, avoiding mortal sin, acting more out of love than with fear, praying to our Lady now and then, honouring her as the Mother of God, yet without having any special devotion to her. The second consists in entertaining for our Lady more perfect feelings of esteem and love, of confidence and veneration. It leads us to join the Confraternities of the Holy Rosary and of the Scapular, to recite the five or the fifteen decades of the Holy Rosary, to honour Mary's images and altars, to publish her praises and to enrol ourselves in her modalities. This devotion is good, holy and praiseworthy if we keep ourselves free from sin. But it is not so perfect as the next, nor so efficient in severing our soul from creatures, in detaching ourselves in order to be united with Jesus Christ. The third devotion to our Lady, known and practiced by very few persons, is this I am about to disclose to you, predestined soul. It consists in giving one's self entirely and as a slave to Mary, and to Jesus through Mary, and after that, to do all that we do, through Mary, with Mary in Mary and for Mary We should choose a special feast day on which we give, consecrate and sacrifice to Mary voluntarily lovingly and without constraint, entirely and without reserve: our body and soul, our exterior property such as house, family and income, and also our interior and spiritual possessions: namely, our merits, graces, virtues, and satisfactions.

PRAYERS

Litany of the Holy Ghost
Litany of the Blessed Virgin Mary (Litany of Loreto)
Ave Maris Stella
St. Louis De Montfort's Prayer to Mary
Pray the Rosary

DAY 22

Today's Reading: *True Devotion to the Blessed Virgin Mary: Nos. 106–110*

Marks of authentic devotion to our Lady

106. First, true devotion to our Lady is interior, that is, it comes from within the mind and the heart and follows from the esteem in which we hold her, the high regard we have for her greatness, and the love we bear her.

107. Second, it is trustful, that is to say, it fills us with confidence in the Blessed Virgin, the confidence that a child has for its loving Mother. It prompts us to go to her in every need of body and soul with great simplicity, trust and affection.

108. Third, true devotion to our Lady is holy, that is, it leads us to avoid sin and to imitate the virtues of Mary. Her ten principal virtues are: deep humility, lively faith, blind obedience, unceasing prayer, constant self-denial, surpassing purity, ardent love, heroic patience, angelic kindness, and heavenly wisdom.

109. Fourth, true devotion to our Lady is constant. It strengthens us in our desire to do good and prevents us from giving up our devotional practices too easily. It gives us the courage to oppose the fashions and maxims of the world, the vexations and unruly inclinations of the flesh and the temptations of the devil. Thus a person truly devoted to our Blessed Lady is not changeable, fretful, scrupulous or timid.

110. Fifth, true devotion to Mary is disinterested. It inspires us to seek God alone in his Blessed Mother and not ourselves. The true subject of Mary does not serve his illustrious Queen for selfish gain. He does not serve her for temporal or eternal well-being but simply and solely because she has the right to be served and God alone in her.

PRAYERS

Litany of the Holy Ghost
Litany of the Blessed Virgin Mary (Litany of Loreto)
Ave Maris Stella
St. Louis De Montfort's Prayer to Mary
Pray the Rosary

DAY 23

Today's Reading: *True Devotion to the Blessed Virgin Mary: Nos. 120–121*

Nature of perfect Devotion to the Blessed Virgin or perfect consecration to Jesus Christ

120. As all perfection consists in our being conformed, united and consecrated to Jesus it naturally follows that the most perfect of all devotions is that which conforms, unites, and consecrates us most completely to Jesus. Now of all God's creatures Mary is the most conformed to Jesus. It therefore follows that, of all devotions, devotion to her makes for the most effective consecration and conformity to him. The more one is consecrated to Mary, the more one is consecrated to Jesus. That is why perfect consecration to Jesus is

but a perfect and complete consecration of oneself to the Blessed Virgin, which is the devotion I teach; or in other words, it is the perfect renewal of the vows and promises of holy baptism.

121. This devotion consists in giving oneself entirely to Mary in order to belong entirely to Jesus through her. It requires us to give:

Our body with its senses and members;

Our soul with its faculties;

Our present material possessions and all we shall acquire in the future;

Our interior and spiritual possessions, that is, our merits, virtues and good actions of the past, the present and the future.

In other words, we give her all that we possess both in our natural life and in our spiritual life as well as everything we shall acquire in the future in the order of nature, of grace, and of glory in heaven. This we do without any reservation, not even of a penny, a hair, or the smallest good deed. And we give for all eternity without claiming or expecting, in return for our offering and our service, any other reward than the honour of belonging to our Lord through Mary and in Mary, even though our Mother were not—as in fact she always is—the most generous and appreciative of all God's creatures.

PRAYERS

Litany of the Holy Ghost
Litany of the Blessed Virgin Mary (Litany of Loreto)

Ave Maris Stella
St. Louis De Montfort's Prayer to Mary
Pray the Rosary

DAY 24

Today's Reading: *True Devotion to the Blessed Virgin Mary:*
Nos. 152–164

This devotion is a smooth, short, perfect and sure way of attaining union with our Lord, in which Christian perfection consists.

(a) This devotion is a smooth way. It is the path which Jesus Christ opened up in coming to us and in which there is no obstruction to prevent us reaching him. It is quite true that we can attain to divine union by other roads, but these involve many more crosses and exceptional setbacks and many difficulties that we cannot easily overcome.

(b) This devotion is a short way to discover Jesus, either because it is a road we do not wander from, or because, as we have just said, we walk along this road with greater ease and joy, and consequently with greater speed. We advance more in a brief period of submission to Mary and dependence on her than in whole years of self-will and self-reliance.

(c) This devotion is a perfect way to reach our Lord and be united to him, for Mary is the most perfect and the most holy of all creatures, and Jesus, who came to us in a perfect manner, chose no other road for his great and wonderful journey. The Most High, the Incomprehensible One, the Inaccessible One, He who is, deigned to come down to us poor earthly creatures who are nothing at all. How was this done? The Most High God came down to us in a perfect way through the humble Virgin Mary, without losing anything of his divinity or holiness. It is likewise through Mary that we poor creatures must ascend to almighty God in a perfect manner without having anything to fear.

(d) This devotion to our Lady is a sure way to go to Jesus and to acquire holiness through union with him. The devotion which I teach is not new. Indeed it could not be condemned without overthrowing the foundations of Christianity. It is obvious then that this devotion is not new. If it is not commonly practised, the reason is that it is too sublime to be appreciated and undertaken by everyone. This devotion is a safe means of going to Jesus Christ, because it is Mary's role to lead us safely to her Son.

PRAYERS

Litany of the Holy Ghost
Litany of the Blessed Virgin Mary (Litany of Loreto)
Ave Maris Stella
St. Louis De Montfort's Prayer to Mary
Pray the Rosary

DAY 25

Today's Reading: *True Devotion to the Blessed Virgin Mary: Nos. 213–225*

Wonderful Effects of this Devotion

213. My dear friend, be sure that if you remain faithful to the interior and exterior practices of this devotion which I will point out, the following effects will be produced in your soul:

1. Knowledge of our unworthiness:

By the light which the Holy Spirit will give you through Mary, his faithful spouse, you will perceive the evil inclinations of your fallen nature and how incapable you are of any good. Finally, the humble Virgin Mary will share her humility with you so that, although you regard yourself with distaste and desire to be disregarded by others, you will not look down slightingly upon anyone.

2. A share in Mary's faith

214. Mary will share her faith with you. Her faith on earth was stronger than that of all the patriarchs, prophets, apostles and saints.

3. The gift of pure love

215. The Mother of fair love will rid your heart of all scruples and inordinate servile fear.

4. Great confidence in God and in Mary

216. Our Blessed Lady will fill you with unbounded confidence in God and in herself: 1) Because you will no longer approach Jesus by yourself but always through Mary, your loving Mother.

5. Communication of the spirit of Mary

217. The soul of Mary will be communicated to you to glorify the Lord. Her spirit will take the place of yours to rejoice in God, her Saviour, but only if you are faithful to the practices of this devotion.

6. Transformation into the likeness of Jesus

218. If Mary, the Tree of Life, is well cultivated in our soul by fidelity to this devotion, she will in due time bring forth her fruit which is none other than Jesus.

7. The greater glory of Christ

222. If you live this devotion sincerely, you will give more glory to Jesus in a month than in many years of a more demanding devotion.

PRAYERS

Litany of the Holy Ghost
Litany of the Blessed Virgin Mary (Litany of Loreto)
Ave Maris Stella
St. Louis De Montfort's Prayer to Mary
Pray the Rosary

DAY 26

Today's Reading: *True Devotion to the Blessed Virgin Mary:*
Nos. 12–38

"If you wish to understand the Mother," says a saint, "then understand the Son. She is a worthy Mother of God." *Hic taceat omnis lingua:* Here let every tongue be silent. My heart has dictated with special joy all that I have written to show that Mary has been unknown up till now, and that that is one of the reasons why Jesus Christ is not known as he should be. If then, as is certain, the knowledge and the kingdom of Jesus Christ must come into the world; it can only be as a necessary consequence of the knowledge and reign of Mary. She who first gave him to the world will establish his kingdom in the world.

With the whole Church I acknowledge that Mary, being a mere creature fashioned by the hands of God is, compared to his infinite majesty, less than an atom, or rather is simply nothing, since he alone can say, "I am he who is." Consequently, this great Lord, who is ever independent and self-sufficient, never had and does not now have any absolute need of the Blessed Virgin for the accomplishment of his will and the manifestation of his glory. To do all things he has only to will them. However, I declare that, considering things as they are, because God has decided to begin and accomplish his greatest works through the Blessed Virgin ever since he created her, we can safely believe that he will not change his plan in the time to come, for he is God and therefore does not change in his thoughts or his way of acting.

Mary is the Queen of heaven and earth by grace as Jesus is king by nature and by conquest. But as the kingdom of Jesus Christ exists primarily in the heart or interior of man, according to the words of the Gospel, "The kingdom of God is within you," so the kingdom of the Blessed Virgin is principally in the interior of man, that is, in his soul. It is principally in souls that she is glorified with her Son more than in any visible creature. So we may call her, as the saints do, Queen of our hearts.

PRAYERS

Litany of the Holy Ghost
Litany of the Blessed Virgin Mary (Litany of Loreto)
Ave Maris Stella
St. Louis De Montfort's Prayer to Mary
Pray the Rosary

WEEK THREE

OBTAIN KNOWLEDGE OF JESUS CHRIST

DURING this period we shall apply ourselves to the study of Jesus Christ. What is to be studied in Christ? First the God-Man, His grace and glory; then His rights to sovereign dominion over us; since, after having renounced Satan and the world, we have taken Jesus Christ for our Lord. What next shall be the object of our study? His exterior actions and also His interior life; namely, the virtues and acts of His Sacred Heart; His association with Mary in the mysteries of the Annunciation and Incarnation, during His infancy and hidden life, at the feast of Cana and on Calvary.

DAY 27

Today's Reading: *True Devotion to the Blessed Virgin Mary: Nos. 61–62*

61. Jesus, our Saviour, true God and true man must be the ultimate end of all our other devotions; otherwise they would be false and misleading. He is the Alpha and the Omega, the beginning and end of everything. "We labour," says St. Paul, "only to make all men perfect in Jesus Christ." For in him alone dwells the entire fullness of the divinity and the complete fullness of grace, virtue and perfection. In him alone we have been blessed with every spiritual blessing; he is the only teacher from whom we must learn; the only Lord on whom we should depend; the only Head to whom we should be united and the only model that we should imitate. He is the only Physician that can heal us; the only Shepherd that can feed us; the only Way that can lead us; the only Truth that we can believe; the only Life that can animate us. He alone is everything to us and he alone can satisfy all our desires. We are given no other name under heaven by which we can be saved. God has laid no other foundation for our salvation, perfection and glory than Jesus. Every edifice which is not built on that firm rock, is founded upon shifting sands and will certainly fall sooner or later. Through him, with him and in him, we can do all things and render all honour and glory to the Father in the unity of the Holy Spirit; we can make ourselves perfect and be for our neighbour a fragrance of eternal life.

62. If then we are establishing sound devotion to our Blessed Lady, it is only in order to establish devotion to our Lord

more perfectly, by providing a smooth but certain way of reaching Jesus Christ. If devotion to our Lady distracted us from our Lord, we would have to reject it as an illusion of the devil. But this is far from being the case. As I have already shown and will show again later on, this devotion is necessary, simply and solely because it is a way of reaching Jesus perfectly, loving him tenderly, and serving him faithfully.

PRAYERS

Litany of the Holy Ghost
Ave Maris Stella
Litany of the Holy Name of Jesus
St. Louis De Montfort's Prayer to Jesus
O Jesus Living in Mary

DAY 28

Today's Reading: *Matthew 26:1, 26–29, 36–46*

And it came to pass, when Jesus had ended all these words, he said to his disciples: You know that after two days shall be the pasch, and the son of man shall be delivered up to be crucified . . .

. . . And whilst they were at supper, Jesus took bread, and blessed, and broke: and gave to his disciples, and said: Take ye, and eat. This is my body. And taking the chalice, he gave thanks, and gave to them, saying: Drink ye all of this. For this is my blood of the new testament, which shall be shed for many unto remission of sins. And I say to you, I will not drink from henceforth of this fruit of the vine, until that day when I shall drink it with you new in the kingdom of my Father . . .

. . . Then Jesus came with them into a country place which is called Gethsemani; and he said to his disciples: Sit you here, till I go yonder and pray. And taking with him Peter and the two sons of Zebedee, he began to grow sorrowful and to be sad. Then he saith to them: My soul is sorrowful even unto death: stay you here, and watch with me. And going a little further, he fell upon his face, praying, and saying: My Father, if it be possible, let this chalice pass from me. Nevertheless not as I will, but as thou wilt. And he cometh to his disciples, and findeth them asleep, and he saith to Peter: What? Could you not watch one hour with me? Watch ye, and pray that ye enter not into temptation. The spirit indeed is willing, but the flesh weak. Again the second time, he went and prayed, saying: My Father, if this chalice may not pass away, but I must drink it, thy will be done. And he cometh again and findeth them sleeping: for their eyes were heavy. And leaving them, he went again: and he prayed the third time, saying the selfsame word. Then he cometh to his disciples, and saith to them: Sleep ye now and take your rest; behold the hour is at hand, and the Son of man shall be betrayed into the hands of sinners. Rise, let us go: behold he is at hand that will betray me.

PRAYERS

Litany of the Holy Ghost
Ave Maris Stella
Litany of the Holy Name of Jesus
St. Louis De Montfort's Prayer to Jesus
O Jesus Living in Mary

DAY 29

Today's Reading: *Imitation of Christ: Book 1, Chapter 1*

Of the Imitation of Christ, and Contempt of all the Vanities of the World

He that followeth Me, walketh not in darkness (John 8:12), saith the Lord. These are the words of Christ, by which we are admonished, how we ought to imitate His life and manners, if we would truly be enlightened, and delivered from all blindness of heart. Let therefore our chiefest endeavour be, to meditate upon the life of Jesus Christ.

The doctrine of Christ exceedeth all the doctrine of holy men.; and he that hath the Spirit will find therein the hidden manna (Apocalypse. 2:17). But it falleth out that many who often hear the Gospel of Christ, feel little desire after it, because they have not the Spirit of Christ (Rom. 8:9). But Whosoever will fully and with relish understand the words of Christ, must endeavor to conform his life wholly to the life of Christ.

What doth it avail thee to discourse profoundly of the Trinity, if thou be void of humility, and art thereby displeasing to the Trinity? Surely profound words do not make a man holy and just; but a virtuous life maketh him dear to God. I had rather feel contrition, than know the definition thereof. If thou didst know the whole Bible by heart, and the sayings of all the philosophers, what would all that profit thee without the love of God (1 Cor. 13:2), and without His grace?

Vanity of vanities, and all is vanity (Eccles. 1:2), except to love God, and to serve Him only. This is the highest wisdom, by contempt of the world to press forward towards heavenly kingdoms.

PRAYERS

Litany of the Holy Ghost
Ave Maris Stella
Litany of the Holy Name of Jesus
St. Louis De Montfort's Prayer to Jesus
O Jesus Living in Mary

DAY 30

Today's Reading: *Matthew 27:36–44*

And they sat and watched him. And they put over his head his cause written: THIS IS JESUS THE KING OF THE JEWS. Then were crucified with him two thieves: one on the right hand, and one on the left. And they that passed by, blasphemed him, wagging their heads, And saying: Vah, thou that destroyest the temple of God, and in three days dost rebuild it: save thy own self: if thou be the Son of God, come down from the cross. In like manner also the chief priests, with the scribes and ancients, mocking, said: He saved others; himself he cannot save. If he be the king of Israel, let him now come down from the cross, and we will believe him. He trusted in God; let him now deliver him if he will have him; for he said: I am the Son of God. And the selfsame thing the thieves also, that were crucified with him, reproached him with.

PRAYERS

Litany of the Holy Ghost
Ave Maris Stella
Litany of the Holy Name of Jesus
St. Louis De Montfort's Prayer to Jesus
O Jesus Living in Mary

DAY 31

Today's Reading: *Imitation of Christ: Book 4, Chapter 2*

That the Great Goodness and Love of God Is Exhibited to Man in This Sacrament

In confidence of Thy goodness and great mercy, O Lord, I draw near, sick to the Healer, hungry and thirsty to the Fountain of life, needy to the King of Heaven, a servant to his Lord, a creature to the Creator, desolate to my own tender Comforter. "But whence is this to me," that Thou comest unto me (Luke 1:43)? What am I, that Thou shouldest grant me Thine own self? how dare a sinner appear before Thee?

And how is it that Thou dost vouchsafe to come unto a sinner? Thou knowest Thy servant, and art well aware that he hath in him no good thing, for which Thou shouldest grant him this. I confess therefore mine own vileness, I acknowledge Thy goodness, I praise Thy tender mercy, and give Thee thanks for Thy transcendent love.

PRAYERS

Litany of the Holy Ghost
Ave Maris Stella
Litany of the Holy Name of Jesus
St. Louis De Montfort's Prayer to Jesus
O Jesus Living in Mary

DAY 32

Today's Reading: *Imitation of Christ: Book 2, Chapter 7*

Of the Love of Jesus above All Things

Blessed is he that understandeth (Psalm 119:1,2) what it is to love Jesus, and to despise himself for Jesus' sake. Thou oughtest to leave thy beloved, for thy beloved (Deut. 6:5; Matt. 22:37; Cant. 2:16); for that Jesus will be loved alone above all things.

The love of things created is deceitful and inconstant; the love of Jesus is faithful and persevering. He that cleaveth unto a creature, shall fall with that which is subject to fall; he that embraceth Jesus shall be made strong for ever.

Love Him, and keep Him for thy friend, who, when all go away, will not forsake thee, nor suffer thee to perish in the end. Some time or other thou must be separated from all, whether thou wilt or no. Keep close to Jesus both in life and in death, and commit thyself unto His faithfulness, who, when all fail, can alone help thee.

Thy Beloved is of that nature, that He will admit of no rival; but will have thy heart alone, and sit on His throne as King.

If thou couldest empty thyself perfectly from all creatures, Jesus would willingly dwell with thee.

True Devotion to the Blessed Virgin Mary: Nos. 257–260

There are some very sanctifying interior practices for those souls who feel called by the Holy Spirit to a high degree of perfection. They may be expressed in four words, doing everything through Mary, with Mary, in Mary, and for Mary, in order to do it more perfectly through Jesus, with Jesus, in Jesus, and for Jesus.

Through Mary

258. We must do everything through Mary, that is, we must obey her always and be led in all things by her spirit, which is the Holy Spirit of God. "Those who are led by the Spirit of God are children of God," says St. Paul. Those who are led by the spirit of Mary are children of Mary, and, consequently children of God, as we have already shown. Among the many servants of Mary only those who are truly and faithfully devoted to her are led by her spirit. I have said that the spirit of Mary is the spirit of God because she was never led by her own spirit, but always by the spirit of God, who made himself master of her to such an extent that he became her very spirit. That is why St. Ambrose says, "May the soul of Mary be in each one of us to glorify the Lord. May the spirit of Mary be in each one of us to rejoice in God." Happy is the man who follows the example of the good Jesuit Brother Rodriguez, who died a holy death, because he will be completely possessed and governed by the spirit of Mary, a spirit which is gentle yet strong, zealous yet prudent, humble yet courageous, pure yet fruitful.

With Mary

260. We must do everything with Mary, that is to say, in all our actions we must look upon Mary, although a simple human being, as the perfect model of every virtue and perfection, fashioned by the Holy Spirit for us to imitate, as far as our limited capacity allows. In every action then we should consider how Mary performed it or how she would perform it if she were in our place. For this reason, we must examine and meditate on the great virtues she practised during her life, especially: 1) Her lively faith, by which she believed the angel's word without the least hesitation, and believed faithfully and constantly even to the foot of the Cross on Calvary. 2) Her deep humility, which made her prefer seclusion, maintain silence, submit to every eventuality and put herself in the last place.

PRAYERS

Litany of the Holy Ghost
Ave Maris Stella
Litany of the Holy Name of Jesus
St. Louis De Montfort's Prayer to Jesus
O Jesus Living in Mary

DAY 33

Today's Reading: *Imitation of Christ: Book 4, Chapter 11*

That the Blood of Christ and the Holy Scriptures Are Most Necessary unto a Faithful Soul

O most sweet Lord Jesus, how great is the pleasure of the devout soul that feasteth with Thee in Thy banquet; where there is set for her no other food to be eaten but Thyself, her only Beloved, and most to be desired above all the desires of her heart! To me also it would be indeed sweet, in Thy presence to pour forth tears from the very bottom of my heart, and with the grateful Magdalene to wash Thy feet with tears (Luke 7:38). But where is that devotion? Where that bountiful flowing of holy tears? Surely in the sight of Thee and Thy holy Angels, my whole heart ought to burn, and to weep for joy. For in this Sacrament I have Thee mystically present, hidden under another shape. For to look upon Thee in Thine own Divine brightness, mine eyes would not be able to endure; nor could even the whole world stand in the splendor of the glory of Thy majesty. Herein then Thou hast regard to my weakness, that Thou dost hide Thyself under this Sacrament.

True Devotion to the Blessed Virgin Mary: Nos. 261–265

In Mary

261. We must do everything in Mary. To understand this we must realise that the Blessed Virgin is the true earthly paradise of the new Adam and that the ancient paradise was only

a symbol of her. There are in this earthly paradise untold riches, beauties, rarities and delights, which the new Adam, Jesus Christ, has left there. It is in this paradise that he "took his delights" for nine months, worked his wonders and displayed his riches with the magnificence of God himself. In this earthly paradise grows the real Tree of Life which bore our Lord, the fruit of Life, the tree of knowledge of good and evil, which bore the Light of the world. In this divine place there are trees planted by the hand of God and watered by his divine unction which have borne and continue to bear fruit that is pleasing to him. Only the Holy Spirit can teach us the truths that these material objects symbolise. 262. The Holy Spirit speaking through the Fathers of the Church, also calls our Lady the Eastern Gate, through which the High Priest, Jesus Christ, enters and goes out into the world. Through this gate he entered the world the first time and through this same gate he will come the second time.

For Mary

265. Finally, we must do everything for Mary. We take Mary for our proximate end, our mysterious intermediary and the easiest way of reaching him. Relying on her protection, we should undertake and carry out great things for our noble Queen. We must defend her privileges when they are questioned and uphold her good name when it is under attack. We must attract everyone, if possible, to her service and to this true and sound devotion. As a reward for these little services, we should expect nothing in return save the honour of belonging to such a lovable Queen and the joy of being united through her to Jesus, her Son, by a bond that is indissoluble in time and in eternity.

PRAYERS

Litany of the Holy Ghost
Ave Maris Stella
Litany of the Holy Name of Jesus
St. Louis De Montfort's Prayer to Jesus
O Jesus Living in Mary

HOW TO MAKE YOUR CONSECRATION

AT THE END of three weeks, we should go to confession and Holy Communion with the intention of giving ourselves to Jesus Christ in the quality of slaves of love, by the hands of Mary. After Communion, we should recite the consecration prayer—we ought to write it, or have it written, and sign it the same day the consecration is made. It would be well that on this day, we should pay some tribute to Jesus Christ and our Blessed Lady, either as a penance for our past unfaithfulness to the vows of Baptism, or as a testimony of dependence on the dominion of Jesus and Mary. This tribute should be one in accordance with your fervour, such as a fast, mortification or alms, or a candle. If but a pin is given in homage, and given with a good heart, it will be enough for Jesus, Who loves only the good will. Once a year at least, and on the same day, we should renew this consecration, observing the same practices during the three weeks.

You should aim to do the consecration on a Marian Feast day, like the Immaculate Conception. Here is a list of prominent Marian Feast days:

January 1—Mary, Mother of God
January 8—Our Lady of Prompt Succor
February 2—Purification of the Virgin

February 11—Our Lady of Lourdes

March 25—Annunciation by Archangel Gabriel (it may be either moved to the day before Palm Sunday should this date be on Holy Week; or to the Monday after the second Sunday of Easter if this date falls on either Friday or Saturday of Holy Week or during Easter Week)

April 26—Our Lady of Good Counsel

May 1—Queen of Heaven

May 13—Our Lady of Fatima

May 24—Mary Help of Christians

May 31—Mary, Mediatrix of all Graces

May 31—Visitation of the Blessed Virgin Mary

June 27—Our Lady of Perpetual Help

July 16—Our Lady of Mount Carmel

August 2—Our Lady of Angels

August 5—Dedication of the Basilica of Saint Mary Major

August 15—Assumption into Heaven

August 21—Our Lady of Knock

August 22—Queenship of Mary

August 22—Black Madonna of Częstochowa

September 8—Nativity of the Blessed Virgin Mary

September 12—The Most Holy Name of the Blessed Virgin Mary

September 15—Our Lady of Sorrows

September 19—Our Lady of La Salette

September 24—Our Lady of Walsingham

October 7—Most Holy Rosary

November 16—Our Lady of Mercy

November 21—Presentation of Mary

December 8—Immaculate Conception

December 12—Our Lady of Guadalupe

1 day after Ascension of Jesus—Our Lady of Apostles

1 day after Pentecost—Our Lady of Holy Church

9 days after Corpus Christi—Immaculate Heart of Mary

CONSECRATION OF OURSELVES TO JESUS CHRIST, THE INCARNATE WISDOM, BY THE HANDS OF MARY

O ETERNAL and Incarnate Wisdom! O sweetest and most Adorable Jesus! True God and True Man, only Son of the Eternal Father, and of Mary always Virgin! I adore Thee profoundly in the bosom and splendours of Thy Father during eternity; and I adore Thee also in the Virginal bosom of Mary, Thy most worthy Mother, in the time of Thine Incarnation.

I give Thee thanks for that Thou hast annihilated Thyself, in taking the form of a slave, in order to rescue me from the cruel slavery of the devil. I praise and glorify Thee for that Thou hast been pleased to submit Thyself to Mary, Thy holy Mother, in all things, in order to make me Thy faithful slave through her. But, alas! ungrateful and faithless as I have been, I have not kept the promises which I made so solemnly to Thee in my Baptism; I have not fulfilled my obligations; I do not deserve to be called Thy son, nor yet Thy slave; and as there is nothing in me which does not merit Thine anger and Thy repulse, I dare no more come by myself before Thy Most Holy and August Majesty. It is on this account that I have recourse to the intercession of Thy most holy Mother, whom Thou hast given me for a mediatrix with Thee. It is by her means that I hope to obtain of Thee contrition, and the pardon of my sins, the acquisition and the preservation of wisdom. I salute thee, then, O immaculate Mary, living tabernacle of the Divinity, where the Eternal Wisdom willed to be hidden, and to be adored by Angels and by men. I hail thee, O Queen of heaven and earth, to whose empire everything is subject which is under God.

I salute thee, O sure refuge of sinners, whose mercy fails to no one. Hear the desires which I have of the Divine Wisdom; and for that end receive the vows and offerings which my lowness presents to thee. I, [*Name*], a faithless sinner—I renew and ratify today in thy hands the vows of my Baptism; I renounce for ever Satan, his pomp's and works; and I give myself entirely to Jesus Christ, the Incarnate Wisdom, to carry my cross after Him all the days of my life, and to be more faithful to Him than I have ever been before.

In the presence of all the heavenly court I choose thee this day for my Mother and Mistress. I deliver and consecrate to thee, as thy slave, my body and soul, my goods, both interior and exterior, and even the value of all my good actions, past, present, and future; leaving to you the entire and full right of disposing of me, and all that belongs to me, without exception, according to thy good pleasure, to the greatest glory of God, in time and in eternity.

Receive, O benignant Virgin, this little offering of my slavery, in the honour of, and in union with, that subjection which the Eternal Wisdom deigned to have to thy Maternity, in homage to the power which both of you have over this little worm and miserable sinner, and in thanksgiving for the privileges with which the Holy Trinity hath favoured thee. I protest that I wish henceforth, as thy true slave, to seek thy honour and to obey thee in all things.

O admirable Mother, present me to thy dear Son as His eternal slave, so that as He hath redeemed me by thee, by thee He may receive me. O Mother of mercy, get me the grace to obtain the true Wisdom of God; and for that end put me in the number of those whom thou lovest, whom thou teachest, whom thou conductest, and whom thou nourishest and protectest, as thy children and thy slaves.

O faithful Virgin, make me in all things so perfect a disciple, imitator, and slave of the Incarnate Wisdom, Jesus Christ thy Son, I may attain, by thy intercession, and by thy example, to the fullness of His age on earth, and of His glory in the heavens. *Amen.*

> Qui potest capere, capiat.
> Let him take who can take.
>
> Quis sapiens, et intelliget haec?
> Who is wise, and he shall understand these things?

PRAYERS

VENI CREATOR SPIRITUS

Come, Holy Spirit, Creator blest,
and in our souls take up Thy rest;
come with Thy grace and heavenly aid
to fill the hearts which Thou hast made.

O comforter, to Thee we cry,
O heavenly gift of God Most High,
O fount of life and fire of love,
and sweet anointing from above.

Thou in Thy sevenfold gifts are known;
Thou, finger of God's hand we own;
Thou, promise of the Father,
Thou Who dost the tongue with power imbue.

Kindle our sense from above,
and make our hearts o'erflow with love;
with patience firm and virtue high
the weakness of our flesh supply.

Far from us drive the foe we dread,
and grant us Thy peace instead;

so shall we not, with Thee for guide,
turn from the path of life aside.

Oh, may Thy grace on us bestow
the Father and the Son to know;
and Thee, through endless times confessed,
of both the eternal Spirit blest.

Now to the Father and the Son,
Who rose from death, be glory given,
with Thou, O Holy Comforter,
henceforth by all in earth and heaven. Amen.

AVE MARIS STELLA

Hail, O Star of the ocean,
God's own Mother blest,
ever sinless Virgin,
gate of heav'nly rest.

Taking that sweet Ave,
which from Gabriel came,
peace confirm within us,
changing Eve's name.

Break the sinners' fetters,
make our blindness day,
Chase all evils from us,
for all blessings pray.

Show thyself a Mother,
may the Word divine
born for us thine Infant

hear our prayers through thine.

Virgin all excelling,
mildest of the mild,
free from guilt preserve us
meek and undefiled.

Keep our life all spotless,
make our way secure
till we find in Jesus,
joy for evermore.

Praise to God the Father,
honor to the Son,
in the Holy Spirit,
be the glory one. Amen.

MAGNIFICAT

My soul doth magnify the Lord. And my spirit hath rejoiced
in God my Saviour. Because He hath regarded the humility
of His handmaid; for behold from henceforth all generations
shall call me Blessed. Because He that is mighty, hath done
great things to me; and Holy is His name. And His mercy is
from generation unto generations, to them that fear Him. He
hath shewed might in His arm: He hath scattered the proud
in the conceit of their heart. He hath put down the mighty
from their seat, and hath exalted the humble. He hath filled
the hungry with good things; and the rich He hath sent
empty away. He hath received Israel his servant, being mindful of his mercy: As He spoke to our fathers, to Abraham and
to His seed for ever. Amen.

GLORY BE

Glory be to the Father, and to the Son, and to the Holy Ghost.

As it was in the beginning, is now, and ever shall be, world without end. Amen.

PRAY THE ROSARY

How to pray the Holy Rosary of the Blessed Virgin Mary:

A sign of the cross on the Crucifix and then the Apostles' Creed;

An Our Father on the first large bead;

A Hail Mary on each of the three small beads with the following intentions (the theological virtues):
For the increase of faith
For the increase of hope
For the increase of charity

A Glory Be to the Father;

Announce the mystery

An "Our Father" on the large bead

A "Hail Mary" on each of the adjacent ten small beads;

A "Glory Be to the Father";

(The Fatima Prayer is commonly added here, as a pious addition: "O My Jesus, Forgive us our sins. Save us from the fires of hell. Lead all souls to Heaven. Especially those most in need of thy mercy.")

Announce the next mystery, again an Our Father on the next large bead, followed by ten Hail Marys on the small beads, the Glory Be to the Father, (and Fatima Prayer) for each of the following decades;

In conclusion, Hail Holy Queen and a sign of the cross.

LITANY OF THE HOLY GHOST

Lord, have mercy on us.
Christ, have mercy on us.
Lord, have mercy on us.

Father all powerful, have mercy on us
Jesus, Eternal Son of the Father, Redeemer of the world, save us.
Spirit of the Father and the Son, boundless life of both, sanctify us.
Holy Trinity, hear us.

Holy Ghost, Who proceedest from the Father and the Son, enter our hearts.
Holy Ghost, Who art equal to the Father and the Son, enter our hearts.

Promise of God the Father, have mercy on us.
Ray of heavenly light, have mercy on us.
Author of all good, have mercy on us.

Source of heavenly water, have mercy on us.
Consuming fire, have mercy on us.
Ardent charity, have mercy on us.
Spiritual unction, have mercy on us.
Spirit of love and truth, have mercy on us.
Spirit of wisdom and understanding, have mercy on us.
Spirit of counsel and fortitude, have mercy on us.
Spirit of knowledge and piety, have mercy on us.
Spirit of the fear of the Lord, have mercy on us.
Spirit of grace and prayer, have mercy on us.
Spirit of peace and meekness, have mercy on us.
Spirit of modesty and innocence, have mercy on us.

Holy Ghost, the Comforter, have mercy on us.
Holy Ghost, the Sanctifier, have mercy on us.
Holy Ghost, Who governest the Church, have mercy on us.
Gift of God, the Most High, have mercy on us.
Spirit Who fillest the universe, have mercy on us.
Spirit of the adoption of the children of God, have mercy on us.

Holy Ghost, inspire us with horror of sin.
Holy Ghost, come and renew the face of the earth.
Holy Ghost, shed Thy light in our souls.
Holy Ghost, engrave Thy law in our hearts.
Holy Ghost, inflame us with the flame of Thy love.
Holy Ghost, open to us the treasures of Thy graces.
Holy Ghost, teach us to pray well.
Holy Ghost, enlighten us with Thy heavenly inspirations.
Holy Ghost, lead us in the way of salvation.
Holy Ghost, grant us the only necessary knowledge.
Holy Ghost, inspire in us the practice of good. Holy Ghost, grant us the merits of all virtues.
Holy Ghost, make us persevere in justice.
Holy Ghost, be Thou our everlasting reward.

Lamb of God, Who takest away the sins of the world, Send us Thy Holy Ghost.

Lamb of God, Who takest away the sins of the world, pour down into our souls the gifts of the Holy Ghost.

Lamb of God, Who takest away the sins of the world, grant us the Spirit of wisdom and piety.

V. Come, Holy Ghost! Fill the hearts of Thy faithful,
R. And enkindle in them the fire of Thy love.

Let Us Pray. Grant, Omerciful Father, that Thy Divine Spirit may enlighten, inflame and purify us, that He may penetrate us with His heavenly dew and make us fruitful in good works, through Our Lord Jesus Christ, Thy Son, Who with Thee, in the unity of the same Spirit, liveth and reigneth forever and ever.

R. Amen.

LITANY OF THE BLESSED VIRGIN MARY
(LITANY OF LORETO)

Lord, have mercy on us,
Christ have mercy on us.
Lord, have mercy on us.

Christ hear us.
Christ, graciously hear us.

God the Father of Heaven, have mercy on us.
God the Son, Redeemer of the world, have mercy on us.
God the Holy Ghost, have mercy on us.
Holy Trinity, One God, have mercy on us.

Holy Mary, pray for us.
Holy Mother of God, pray for us.
Holy Virgin of virgins, pray for us.
Mother of Christ, pray for us.
Mother of divine grace, pray for us.
Mother most pure, pray for us.
Mother most chaste, pray for us.
Mother inviolate, pray for us.
Mother undefiled, pray for us.
Mother most amiable, pray for us.
Mother most admirable, pray for us.
Mother of good counsel,pray for us.
Mother of our Creator, pray for us.
Mother of our Saviour, pray for us.
Mother of the Church, pray for us.
Virgin most prudent, pray for us.
Virgin most venerable, pray for us.
Virgin most renowned, pray for us.
Virgin most powerful, pray for us.
Virgin most merciful, pray for us.
Virgin most faithful, pray for us.
Preparation for Consecration, pray for us.
Mirror of justice, pray for us.
Seat of wisdom, pray for us.
Cause of our joy, pray for us.
Vessel of honor, pray for us.
Singular vessel of devotion, pray for us.
Mystical rose, pray for us.
Tower of David, pray for us.
Tower of ivory, pray for us.
House of gold, pray for us.
Ark of the covenant, pray for us.
Gate of Heaven, pray for us.
Morning star, pray for us.

Health of the sick, pray for us.
Refuge of sinners, pray for us.
Comforter of the afflicted, pray for us.
Help of Christians, pray for us.
Queen of angels, pray for us.
Queen of patriarchs, pray for us.
Queen of prophets, pray for us.
Queen of Apostles, pray for us.
Queen of martyrs, pray for us.
Queen of confessors, pray for us.
Queen of virgins, pray for us.
Queen of all saints, pray for us.
Queen conceived without Original Sin, pray for us.
Queen assumed into Heaven, pray for us.
Queen of the most holy Rosary, pray for us.
Queen of peace, pray for us.

Lamb of God, Who takest away the sins of the world, Spare us, O Lord.
Lamb of God, Who takest away the sins of the world, Graciously hear us, O Lord.
Lamb of God, Who takest away the sins of the world, Have mercy on us.

V. Pray for us, O holy Mother of God,
R. That we may be made worthy of the promises of Christ.

Let Us Pray. Grant, we beseech Thee, O Lord God, unto us Thy servants, that we may rejoice in continual health of mind and body, and by the glorious intercession of Blessed Mary, ever virgin, may be delivered from present sadness, and enter into the joy of Thine eternal gladness. Through Christ Our Lord.

R. Amen

LITANY OF THE HOLY NAME OF JESUS

Lord, have mercy on us.
Christ, have mercy on us.
Lord, have mercy on us. Jesus, hear us.
Jesus, graciously hear us.

God the Father of Heaven, have mercy on us.
God the Son, Redeemer of the world, have mercy on us.
God the Holy Ghost, have mercy on us.
Holy Trinity, One God, have mercy on us.
Jesus, Son of the living God, have mercy on us.
Jesus, splendor of the Father, have mercy on us.
Jesus, brightness of eternal light, have mercy on us.
Jesus, King of glory, have mercy on us.
Jesus, sun of justice, have mercy on us.
Jesus, Son of the Virgin Mary, have mercy on us.
Jesus, most amiable, have mercy on us.
Jesus, most admirable, have mercy on us.
Jesus, mighty God, have mercy on us.
Jesus, Father of the world to come, have mercy on us.
Jesus, angel of great counsel, have mercy on us.
Jesus, most powerful, have mercy on us.
Jesus, most patient, have mercy on us.
Jesus, most obedient, have mercy on us.
Jesus, meek and humble, have mercy on us.
Jesus, lover of chastity, have mercy on us.
Jesus, lover of us, have mercy on us.
Jesus, God of peace, have mercy on us.
Jesus, author of life, have mercy on us.
Jesus, model of virtues, have mercy on us.
Jesus, lover of souls, have mercy on us.

Jesus, our God, have mercy on us.
Jesus, our refuge, have mercy on us.
Jesus, Father of the poor, have mercy on us.
Jesus, treasure of the faithful, have mercy on us.
Jesus, Good Shepherd, have mercy on us.
Jesus, true light, have mercy on us.
Jesus, eternal wisdom, have mercy on us.
Jesus, infinite goodness, have mercy on us.
Jesus, our way and our life, have mercy on us.
Jesus, joy of angels, have mercy on us.
Jesus, King of patriarchs, have mercy on us.
Jesus, master of Apostles, have mercy on us.
Jesus, teacher of Evangelists, have mercy on us.
Jesus, strength of martyrs, have mercy on us.
Jesus, light of confessors, have mercy on us.
Jesus, purity of virgins, have mercy on us.
Jesus, crown of all saints, have mercy on us.

Be merciful, spare us, O Jesus.
Be merciful, graciously hear us, O Jesus.

From all evil, Jesus, deliver us.
From mall sin, Jesus, deliver us.
From Thy wrath, Jesus, deliver us.
From the snares of the devil, Jesus, deliver us.
From the spirit of fornication, Jesus, deliver us.
From everlasting death, Jesus, deliver us.
From the neglect of Thine inspirations, Jesus, deliver us.

Through the mystery of Thy holy Incarnation, Jesus, deliver
us.
Through Thy nativity, Jesus, deliver us.
Through Thine infancy, Jesus, deliver us.
Through Thy most divine life, Jesus, deliver us.
Through Thy labors, Jesus, deliver us.

Through Thine agony and Passion, Jesus, deliver us.
Through Thy cross and dereliction, Jesus, deliver us.
Through Thy sufferings, Jesus, deliver us.
Through Thy death and burial, Jesus, deliver us.
Through Thy Resurrection, Jesus, deliver us.
Through Thine Ascension, Jesus, deliver us.
Through Thine institution of the most Holy Eucharist, Jesus, deliver us.
Through Thy joys, Jesus, deliver us.
Through Thy glory, Jesus, deliver us.

Lamb of God, Who takest away the sins of the world, Spare us, O Jesus.
Lamb of God, Who takest away the sins of the world, Graciously hear us, O Jesus.
Lamb of God, Who takest away the sins of the world, Have mercy on us.

Jesus, hear us,
Jesus, graciously hear us.

Let Us Pray. O Lord Jesus Christ, Who hast said: Ask and ye shall receive, seek and ye shall find, knock and it shall be opened unto you; grant, we beseech Thee, to us who ask the gift of Thy divine love, that we may ever love Thee with all our hearts, and in all our words and actions, and never cease from praising Thee.

Give us, O Lord, a perpetual fear and love of Thy holy Name; for Thou never failest to govern those whom Thou dost solidly establish in Thy love, Who livest and reignest world without end.

R. Amen.

ST. LOUIS DE MONTFORT'S PRAYER TO MARY

Hail Mary, beloved Daughter of the Eternal Father! Hail Mary, admirable Mother of the Son! Hail Mary, faithful spouse of the Holy Ghost! Hail Mary, my dear Mother, my loving Mistress, my powerful sovereign! Hail my joy, my glory, my heart and my soul! Thou art all mine by mercy, and I am all thine by justice. But I am not yet sufficiently thine. I now give myself wholly to thee without keeping anything back for myself or others. If thou still seest in me anything which does not belong to thee, I beseech thee to take it and to make thyself the absolute Mistress of all that is mine. Destroy in me all that may be displeasing to God, root it up and bring it to nought; place and cultivate in me everything that is pleasing to thee.

May the light of thy faith dispel the darkness of my mind; may thy profound humility take the place of my pride; may thy sublime contemplation check the distractions of my wandering imagination; may thy continuous sight of God fill my memory with His presence; may the burning love of thy heart inflame the lukewarmness of mine; may thy virtues take the place of my sins; may thy merits be my only adornment in the sight of God and make up for all that is wanting in me. Finally, dearly beloved Mother, grant, if it be possible, that I may have no other spirit but thine to know Jesus and His divine will; that I may have no other soul but thine to praise and glorify the Lord; that I may have no other heart but thine to love God with a love as pure and ardent as thine I do not ask thee for visions, revelations, sensible devotion or spiritual pleasures. It is thy privilege to see God clearly; it is thy privilege to enjoy heavenly bliss; it is thy privilege to triumph gloriously in Heaven at the right hand of thy Son and to hold absolute sway over angels, men and demons; it is thy privilege to dispose of all the gifts of God, just as thou willest.

Such is, O heavenly Mary, the "best part," which the Lord has given thee and which shall never be taken away from thee-and this thought fills my heart with joy. As for my part here below, I wish for no other than that which was thine: to believe sincerely without spiritual pleasures; to suffer joyfully without human consolation; to die continually to myself without respite; and to work zealously and unselfishly for thee until death as the humblest of thy servants. The only grace I beg thee to obtain for me is that every day and every moment of my life I may say: Amen, so be it's all that thou didst do while on earth; Amen, so be it's all that thou art now doing in Heaven; Amen, so be it-to all that thou art doing in my soul, so that thou alone mayest fully glorify Jesus in me for time and eternity. Amen.

ST. LOUIS DE MONTFORT'S PRAYER TO JESUS

O most loving Jesus, deign to let me pour forth my gratitude before Thee, for the grace Thou hast bestowed upon me in giving me to Thy holy Mother through the devotion of Holy Bondage, that she may be my advocate in the presence of Thy majesty and my support in my extreme misery. Alas, O Lord! I am so wretched that without this dear Mother I should be certainly lost. Yes, Mary is necessary for me at Thy side and everywhere: that she may appease Thy just wrath, because I have so often offended Thee; that she may save me from the eternal punishment of Thy justice, which I deserve;

that she may contemplate Thee, speak to Thee, pray to Thee, approach Thee and please Thee; that she may help me to save my soul and the souls of others; in short, Mary is necessary for me that I may always do Thy holy will and seek Thy greater glory in all things. Ah, would that I could proclaim throughout the whole world the mercy that Thou hast shown to me! Would that everyone might know I should be already damned, were it not for Mary! Would that I might offer worthy thanksgiving for so great a blessing! Mary is in me. Oh, what a treasure! Oh, what a consolation! And shall I not be entirely hers'? Oh, what ingratitude! My dear Saviour, send me death rather than such a calamity, for I would rather die than live without belonging entirely to Mary. With St. John the Evangelist at the foot of the Cross, I have taken her a thousand times for my own and as many times have given myself to her; but if I have not yet done it as Thou, dear Jesus, dost wish, I now renew this offering as Thou dost desire me to renew it. And if Thou seest in my soul or my body anything that does not belong to this august princess, I pray Thee to take it and cast it far from me, for whatever in me does not belong to Mary is unworthy of Thee. O Holy Spirit, grant me all these graces. Plant in my soul the Tree of true Life, which is Mary; cultivate it and tend it so that it may grow and blossom and bring forth the fruit of life in abundance. O Holy Spirit, give me great devotion to Mary, Thy faithful spouse; give me great confidence in her maternal heart and an abiding refuge in her mercy, so that by her Thou mayest truly form in me Jesus Christ, great and mighty, unto the fullness of His perfect age. Amen.

O JESUS LIVING IN MARY

O Jesus living in Mary,
Come and live in Thy servants,
In the spirit of Thy holiness,
In the fullness of Thy might,
In the truth of Thy virtues,
In the perfection of Thy ways,
In the communion of Thy mysteries;
Subdue every hostile power
In Thy spirit, for the glory of the Father. Amen.

CATHOLIC WAY PUBLISHING

QUALITY PAPERBACKS AND E-BOOKS

True Devotion to Mary: With Preparation for Total Consecration
by Saint Louis de Montfort
6" x 9" Hardback:..ISBN–13: 978-1-78379-004-3
6" x 9" Paperback: ISBN–13: 978-1-78379-011-1
5" x 8" Paperback: ISBN–13: 978-1-78379-000-5
MOBI E-Book:..ISBN–13: 978-1-78379-001-2
EPUB E-Book: ISBN–13: 978-1-78379-002-9

The Secret of the Rosary by Saint Louis de Montfort
5" x 8" Paperback: ISBN–13: 978-1-78379-310-5
MOBI E-Book:..ISBN–13: 978-1-78379-311-2
EPUB E-Book: ISBN–13: 978-1-78379-312-9

The Imitation of Christ by Thomas a Kempis
5" x 8" Paperback: ISBN–13: 978-1-78379-037-1
MOBI E-Book:..ISBN–13: 978-1-78379-038-8
EPUB E-Book: ISBN–13: 978-1-78379-039-5

My Daily Prayers by Catholic Way Publishing
5" x 8" Paperback: ISBN–13: 978-1-78379-027-2
MOBI E-Book:..ISBN–13: 978-1-78379-028-9
EPUB E-Book: ISBN–13: 978-1-78379-029-6

The Mystical City of God: Popular Abridgement
by Venerable Mary of Agreda
5" x 8" Paperback: ISBN–13: 978-1-78379-063-0
MOBI E-Book:..ISBN–13: 978-1-78379-064-7
EPUB E-Book: ISBN–13: 978-1-78379-065-4

The Three Ages of the Interior Life: Prelude of Eternal Life
by Reverend Reginald Garrigou-Lagrange O.P.
6" x 9" Paperback Volume 1:............................ISBN–13: 978-1-78379-378-5
6" x 9" Paperback Volume 2:............................ISBN–13: 978-1-78379-379-2
MOBI E-Book:..ISBN–13: 978-1-78379-376-1
EPUB E-Book: ISBN–13: 978-1-78379-377-8

www.catholicwaypublishing.com
London, England, UK
2013

Made in the USA
Thornton, CO
10/04/24 22:16:26

3f18ecb1-b17f-4f1e-84b2-57159c4435e2R01